Severin Bischof and Thomas Rudolph
Consumer Goods Subscriptions

Severin Bischof
and Thomas Rudolph

Consumer Goods Subscriptions

How to Win in Retail in the 21st Century

DE GRUYTER

The authors would like to thank Dr. Mark Kyburz for his support regarding the translation of parts of our research and Michael Hoang for his support in the revision of this manuscript.

ISBN 978-3-11-073511-6
e-ISBN (PDF) 978-3-11-073019-7
e-ISBN (EPUB) 978-3-11-073026-5

Library of Congress Control Number: 2021941699

Bibliographic information published by the Deutsche Nationalbibliothek
The Deutsche Nationalbibliothek lists this publication in the Deutsche Nationalbibliografie; detailed bibliographic data are available on the internet at http://dnb.dnb.de.

www.degruyter.com

Contents

Preface

Subscriptions offer new opportunities for businesses because consumers are increasingly intrigued by the idea of automating their consumption. Retail subscriptions achieve exactly this objective by enabling consumers to make recurring purchases of goods and services without having to intervene. We argue that adapting to this change in consumer behavior allows retailers to increase customer loyalty and corporate success. Our book aims to help retail managers attract consumers with innovative subscription models and thereby leverage hitherto unexploited sales potential.

This book summarizes our research findings and publications on a relatively recent phenomenon: consumer goods subscriptions. We interpret this innovation from a business perspective and provide insights, both conceptual and practical, from an entrepreneurial perspective. Our book draws on several of our most recent publications: Severin Bischof's doctoral thesis (Bischof, 2019); a managerial book published by Springer (Bischof and Rudolph, 2020); academic papers in the *Journal of Retailing and Consumer Services* (Bischof, Boettger, and Rudolph, 2020) and the *Marketing Review St. Gallen* (Rudolph, Bischof, Boettger and Weiler, 2017); various publications in conference proceedings (Bischof, Boettger, and Rudolph, 2020; Bischof, Boettger, and Rudolph, 2019; Bischof, Scheidegger, Boettger, and Rudolph 2019; Bischof, Rudolph, Scheidegger, and Boettger, 2018; Bischof, Boettger, and Rudolph, 2017); and a representative market study conducted in German-speaking Switzerland on the status quo of retail subscriptions (Rudolph, Bischof, and Schuerch, 2018). It also taps into various of the authors' commentaries on present-day activities in the subscription industry that were featured in public media (Bischof, Rudolph, and Hauschke, 2020; Guentert, 2019, June 20; Guentert, 2019, June 24; Guentert, 2020, May 7; Guentert, 2020, September 11).

This book takes into account the views of consumers and managers on this new phenomenon. It offers concise and trenchant insight into retail subscriptions and supports managers in introducing subscription services through a wealth of practical advice, tools, and models. Various company examples illustrate our empirical findings and should inspire readers to introduce subscriptions in their companies.

We hope that the interested reader, in addition to recognizing the opportunities arising from subscriptions, will realize the challenges posed by subscriptions and be able to maintain a balanced view. The subscription market is still in its infancy. Importantly, subscriptions are not surefire successes. Exploiting their potential requires market and customer proximity, substantial sensitivity, and a focus on innovativeness.

St. Gallen, May 2021

https://doi.org/10.1515/9783110730197-203

1 Introduction

When was the last time that you bought a song as an MP3 file? This probably seems as obsolete as buying a CD, let alone a vinyl record. Mind you . . . the latter are currently experiencing a small renaissance. But let us not digress. The fact is that you are probably using one of the more common streaming services (e.g., Spotify, Apple Music, or Deezer) to listen to your favorite music. Presumably, you will not even notice that you are no longer paying to listen to (i.e., consume) a single song; that, to be sure, is a thing of the past. Paying monthly flat rates has probably become so burdensome that you consider regular charges such as your Netflix streaming subscription to be perfectly normal. The point is that exactly this subscription mechanism is spreading rapidly in today's consumer society – and there is no end in sight.

"Subscriptioning" is spreading like wildfire. For example, Porsche enables consumers to drive a wide range of Porsche sports cars in selected US cities if they take out a monthly "Porsche Drive" subscription starting at $2,100 (Porsche, 2021). Depending on whether consumers need a convertible (for a beach trip) or a sport utility vehicle (SUV) (for a skiing holiday), the Porsche subscription offers the same flexibility. Compared to the approximately $1,000 needed to lease a Porsche Cayenne, the subscription provider charges handsomely for this flexibility – the subscription requires neither a minimum term nor a 20 percent deposit on the vehicle price. This raises a ticklish question: Do subscriptions pay off for companies at all?

Subscriptions can be very profitable. IKEA is currently testing various forms of furniture subscriptions (Guentert, 2019). In Switzerland, consumers can subscribe to full-scale office furnishing packages – based on what we call "Easy In, Hard Out." From the customer's point of view, paying IKEA smaller monthly subscription fees is more attractive than large one-off payments. Subscriptions reduce initial investment and create a cost-effective entry point: "Easy In." IKEA enables subscription customers to buy furniture as their own property at any time at the full price. A discount is offered depending on the period of use. However, as the subscription period increases, and with payments effected, it is no longer worth buying the furniture. This is the case, for example, if subscription payments exceed the value of the furniture after one or two years. After two years, only continuing the subscription makes sense: "Hard Out." Its subscription model could therefore prove to be extremely profitable for IKEA, depending on the duration and intensity of use.

Subscriptions can also be used as complementary services – to add value to assortments or products. One example is Amazon Prime, which 82 percent of all

https://doi.org/10.1515/9783110730197-001

US households with an income of more than $112,000 have already subscribed to (Molla, 2017). The revenue that Amazon generates with this subscription for additional services such as express delivery or media offers is estimated at up to $20 billion for 2020 (Berg and Knights, 2019, p. 39). The New York-based company Peloton not only sells exercise bikes; it also operates a streaming service that allows fitness courses led by professional athletes to be played on the bike's screen (Peloton, 2019). Obviously, the monthly $39 fee for the streaming service is added to the already impressive c. $2,000 to purchase the bike. You, too, may have discovered one or the other offer that could also make your life a little easier.

But do not stop just yet. Subscriptions are now spreading to – and beginning to conquer – the last bastion of consumer society: retail. Do not many of us sometimes dream of forgoing everyday chores – the weekly shopping or buying clothes – to have more time for our families or to enjoy the weekend without extra burdens? This thought has probably frequently crossed your mind – as it has ours. Zalon, Zalando's curated shopping service, allows us to outsource searching for new outfits entirely to our personal stylist and to regularly receive fashion tailored to our needs.

Now if you believe that subscriptions are merely a panacea for simplifying shopping and therefore little else than a modern bellhop for unloved activities, you may wish to note – with all due respect – that you are mistaken. Subscriptions are at times even a source of inspiration, especially if they contain a surprise mechanism. For instance, the GLOSSYBOX cosmetics subscription regularly supplies the latest products and information about the latest trends. With regard to the consequences of Covid-19 we expect a boosting demand for subscriptions; consumers will shop and consume more often at home and will favor subscription services mostly because of convenience and health-related reasons.

What follows examines the phenomenon of subscriptions in our economy. We show the ways in which subscriptions to physical consumer goods differ from digital subscriptions. Since physical consumer goods are not digital, easily scalable products, different services need different orchestration to make subscriptions profitable. We show how best to use subscriptions to expand your client-facing service offering and to make your customer relationships even more exciting.

1.1 Relevance of subscriptions in retail

For some time, more subscription providers (e.g., OUTFITTERY or HelloFresh) have been sending their customers not only recurring deliveries of consumer goods but also at regular intervals.

The subscription model is a new business model that is gaining popularity among consumers and investors alike. Subscriptions are agreements between companies and consumers on recurring deliveries of products and services (Grewal, Roggeveen, and Nordfält, 2017; Reinartz, 2016). When Dollar Shave Club, a razor blade subscription provider, was acquired by consumer goods giant Unilever for $1 billion in 2016, this was widely seen as confirmation of the relevance of subscriptions. This development marks another milestone in the technology-induced transformation of the retail industry – from the physical dimension to the digital world (Grewal, Roggeveen, Compeau, and Levy, 2012; Kumar and Reinartz, 2016; Shankar and Yadav, 2011).

However, subscriptions are suited to purchasing not only consumer goods (e.g., razor blades or socks), but also hedonic goods (e.g., cosmetics, jewelry, and fashion). A McKinsey study identified an annual market growth of more than 100 percent for subscriptions (Chen, Fenyo, Yang, and Zhang, 2018). Consumer goods subscriptions in the United States already generated sales worth approximately $2.6 billion in 2016 (Chen, Fenyo, Yang, and Zhang, 2018). A small number of only 57 consumer goods subscription providers had received a total of $1.4 billion in venture capital by 2016 (CB Insights, 2016). The number of subscription providers is steadily increasing in various categories (e.g., cosmetics, fashion, food, beverages, as well as decorations and home furnishings). Cratejoy, a marketplace for different subscription providers in the US, features more than 2,700 subscription boxes (Cratejoy, 2018). These numerous examples attest to the increasing attractiveness of consumer goods subscriptions, not least because they promise higher profits. A survey of 293 US, UK, and Australian executives (conducted by the market research organization *The Economist* Intelligence Unit) found that 40 percent of companies were working on introducing subscriptions and subscription models as early as 2013 (*The Economist* 2013). In this study, subscriptions thus outperformed rental or leasing models, which were used by only 27 percent and 17 percent of managers, respectively (see Figure 1.1). Despite this very optimistic assessment, let us maintain some critical distance. We do not see subscriptions as a panacea for sales problems in today's economy. Under certain circumstances, however, companies can offer consumers better solutions – ones that are not only economically viable but also stimulate how we might tackle today's pressing climate and environmental issues.

Subscriptions look back on a long history and are certainly not a completely new phenomenon (Baxter 2015; Janzer, 2015; Warrilow, 2015). Remember, for example, the milkman or milkwoman, still popular in the last century, who regularly delivered milk to the front door. Long before that, in the Middle Ages, subscriptions were offered for geographical maps recording the constant changing of borders due to feuds and wars.

We intend to complement the way we distribute goods and services by integrating the following services:

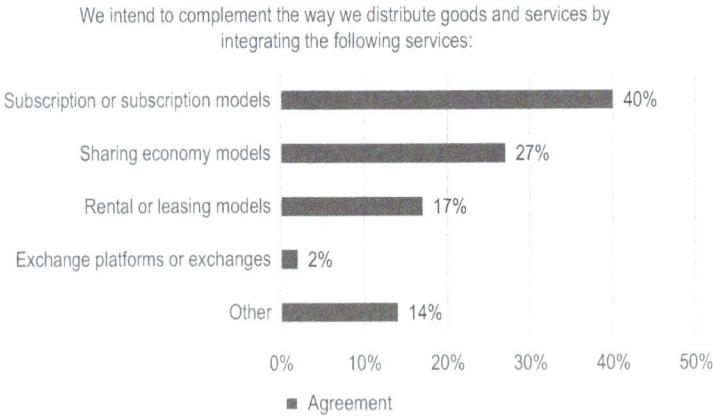

Subscription or subscription models	40%
Sharing economy models	27%
Rental or leasing models	17%
Exchange platforms or exchanges	2%
Other	14%

■ Agreement

Figure 1.1: The importance of new consumption models.
Source: *The Economist* (2013)

In modern times, Blacksocks was one of the first companies to introduce the subscription model to the Swiss market. Blacksocks has been supplying its subscribers with socks selected by customers or chosen by the company themselves since 1990. But it was not until the beginning of the second decade of the 21st century that this revenue model became increasingly established in the area of physical consumer goods (see Figure 1.2). Subscriptions have since developed into an interesting alternative to the so-called "one-off purchase" of goods and services.

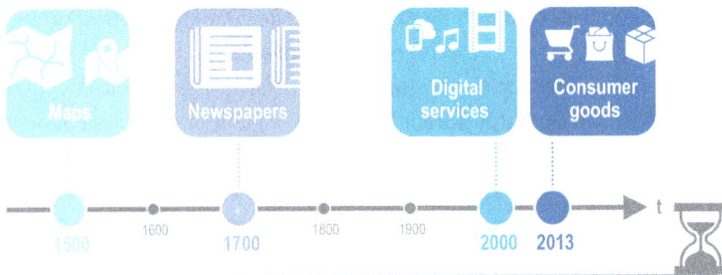

Figure 1.2: Development of subscriptions.
Source: Rudolph, Bischof, Boettger, and Weiler (2017)

The emergence of subscriptions is driven by a fundamental change in consumer behavior: Today, consumers expect ever greater convenience, which subscriptions can offer due to their automatisms. Consumers also seek ever greater inspiration, which subscriptions can provide via surprise mechanisms. Many consumers have meanwhile encountered the various benefits of subscriptions. Our 2018 representative customer survey showed that 30 percent of all German-speaking Swiss had already purchased a product subscription at some point. A total of 18 percent had an active subscription at the time of survey (Rudolph, Bischof, and Schürch, 2019). This figure is on par with the US, where roughly 15 percent of consumers bought a product subscription in 2017.

Subscribers belong to the "Early Market" (so-called "Innovators" and "Early Adopters"), that is, consumers who like to try out new offers. In addition, the risk propensity of subscribers is significantly higher than that of non-subscribers. Subscribers tend to be younger and have a higher gross household income. They see themselves as market and product experts, tend to be more risk-averse, and consider shopping to be more of an adventure. Men tend to be more interested in self-determined automated purchasing (e.g., razor blade subscriptions), while hedonic subscriptions with a surprise factor (e.g., cosmetics surprise boxes) are increasingly bought by women.

Although most subscriptions are offered by start-ups and small businesses, various providers are already achieving a high level of awareness. In 2018, just under half of our German Swiss respondents had heard of the 10 largest subscription providers. Individual providers such as Mondovino (69 percent) or OUTFITTERY (80 percent) achieve above-average awareness levels. The remaining providers also achieve considerable awareness levels, which average about 35 percent for the top 10 subscription providers.

But the subscription business is not easy. Many providers suffer from high churn (i.e., attrition) rates. Blue Apron, an American subscription provider that sends weekly food and recipe packages, is expected to lose 50 percent of its subscribers after the second delivery (Kessler, 2016). Although this figure has not been confirmed by the company, the high churn rate, in addition to customer acquisition, is a major problem. Other sources estimate the churn rate of food subscriptions at approximately 10 percent, and those of digital subscriptions such as Netflix and Spotify at only 1 percent and 5 percent, respectively (*The Economist*, 2018). But customer acquisition also raises many unresolved questions. Subscription providers invest large sums of money by offering high discounts on orders, which reduces profitability. Discount and advertising costs hardly allow making profits at present.

It is therefore hardly surprising that many subscription providers were unable to meet their investors' economic expectations. A total of 13 percent of all subscription providers that emerged in recent years have already filed for bankruptcy (Segran, 2018). HelloFresh, a supplier of food boxes, had to defer its Initial Public Offering (IPO) in 2015 to 2017 at a value of $2.6 billion. In 2020 HelloFresh became profitable based on heavy back wind from Covid-19. A more recent victim is the Swiss market, where Lidl announced the end of its Lidl Menü-box in February 2019. Similar to HelloFresh, Lidl offered its subscribers weekly changing recipes, created by a celebrity chef, together with the necessary ingredients. Presumably, interest in buying was too low. After all, as our study shows, half of Swiss-German respondents knew about the Lidl menu box, but only 2 percent decided to buy it. The purchase completion rate was far too low in relation to advertising expenditure.

The lessons learned from many failed attempts can be summarized in three points. First, subscriptions must meet a relevant need. Demand must exist on the customer side. Only if this is the case, companies should consider introducing subscriptions. Second, launching and operating subscriptions takes much perseverance. Companies should be prepared to optimize their offering and plan for the long term. Third, existing products should be marketed innovatively to arouse and enhance customer interest. We distinguish four types of subscription offers to account for these factors.

Each of these four types promises consumers a different benefit. Subscriptions take surprising and less surprising forms. For some offers, consumers specifically select the subscription content themselves, whereas in the case of surprise boxes the content is unknown. We therefore first describe the basic fields of application and working mechanisms of subscriptions. We also offer valuable suggestions on the phenomenon of surprise, which plays a key role in some basic types of subscriptions. Surprise can quickly overwhelm customers. Thus, the right dose determines whether a subscription will satisfy customers in the long term or whether it is cancelled after the first delivery. This condensed account of our research offers a scientifically sound *and* practice-oriented perspective on an exciting and influential phenomenon of today's economy: subscriptions.

1.2 Empirical studies

In this book, we summarize the results of two empirical studies: a quantitative survey of 568 consumers on their subscription experiences (Rudolph, Bischof, and Schuerch, 2019) and a qualitative management survey among managing directors of international subscription providers (Rudolph, Bischof, Boettger, and Weiler, 2017). The participants in our quantitative consumer study came from German-speaking Switzerland and were representative of the local population in terms of income, age, and gender. They were recruited via an online panel of a renowned market research company. The qualitative management study interviewed seven executives from various successful international subscription companies in three retail sectors (food, fashion, and cosmetics).

The findings of both studies are not limited to specific product groups, but also provide general findings on retail subscriptions. Our analyses include relational statements, for example, between different types of subscribers, and thus offer generalizable findings (i.e., not limited to Switzerland). In particular, the insights into subscriber behavior, together with Swiss consumers' actual usage and purchasing behavior, enable a holistic view of different basic types of subscriptions.

1.3 Structure of this book

Subscriptions are new in retail. We therefore consider both the consumer and the management perspective and provide a holistic view of how subscriptions work.

Chapters 1 and 2 outline the four basic types of retail subscriptions. Subscriptions can be distinguished along two dimensions: the degree of surprise and the degree of personalization. The four types of subscription we have identified satisfy different customer needs and require different levels of business expertise. For example, a provider with a curated surprise mechanism must meet the individual tastes of each customer, whereas a general surprise subscription without a personalization aspect neither makes such an individual promise to customers nor requires the same customer-specific effort.

Chapter 3 considers the main characteristics of subscribers. We compare their general characteristics with those of consumers who have so far avoided subscriptions. We identify acute purchase barriers that provide a realistic perspective on the application areas of subscriptions. Because of their novelty, subscriptions, at least for the time being, appeal to particularly risk-taking adventurers and category experts.

Chapter 4 presents a six-level framework model for the implementation of subscriptions. In line with our intention to combine both management and consumer perspectives, our framework model enables companies to derive their strategy according to their expertise and their customers' needs. Needs-based selection of the respective subscription type allows companies to introduce subscriptions that visibly enhance their service character.

Chapter 5 presents and outlines several case studies of international subscription providers that have successfully innovated their product category's way of retailing via subscriptions. This section of our book allows for a detailed view on subscription providers' success factors and satisfies the reader's curiosity for a portrayal of fruitful business applications of this retailing method. The chapter extends the scope of this book by showcasing not only consumer-facing B2C-subscriptions, but also business-facing B2B-subscriptions with significant momentum.

2 Four basic types of subscriptions

As mentioned, the subscription market comprises many suppliers. In the US alone, the subscription marketplace totals more than 2,700 providers (Cratejoy, 2018). These providers sometimes differ greatly, which warrants the creation of a typology. In order to illustrate the differences between subscription types, we occasionally draw on the results of our recent subscription study (Rudolph, Bischof, and Schuerch, 2019; see Chapter 1, Section 1.2). Our research provides representative findings on subscription usage in German-speaking Switzerland.

For reasons of uniformity and comparability, our typology only describes subscriptions that are aimed at direct purchases of physical consumer goods. Only this approach enables creating a trade-related typology that does not overlap with digital subscription services such as Spotify or Netflix. Digital subscriptions are subject to other mechanisms such that, on the one hand, they do not incur additional marginal costs whereas, on the other, they can be used by all consumers simultaneously. Neither factor applies to physical products.

2.1 Subscription typology

Our typology (see Figure 2.1) takes up the surprise and benefit-related arguments of previous subscription typologies, which have so far only been considered separately (Bischof, Boettger, and Rudolph, 2019). It has two dimensions: the degree of surprise and the degree of personalization. Regarding the degree of surprise, a subscription can be more experience-oriented or transactional, depending on whether it includes a surprise mechanism or not. Regarding the personalization level, providers assume that buyers have either specific personal expectations or unspecific needs, depending on whether the subscription's product content is tailored to individual customer preferences or not.

Our typology has four quadrants and thus comprises four basic subscription types: Predefined, Access, Curated, and Surprise. A predefined subscription is a transactional and personalized subscription because buyers predefine a product that they receive at regular intervals. An access subscription is also transactional but less personalized, because buyers do not know which products they can purchase prior to subscribing. Access subscriptions enable purchasing specific products that are unpurchasable without a subscription. They thus require greater willingness to purchase a variety of products. Surprise and curated subscriptions are both experience-oriented by offering surprises. Contrary to surprise

https://doi.org/10.1515/9783110730197-002

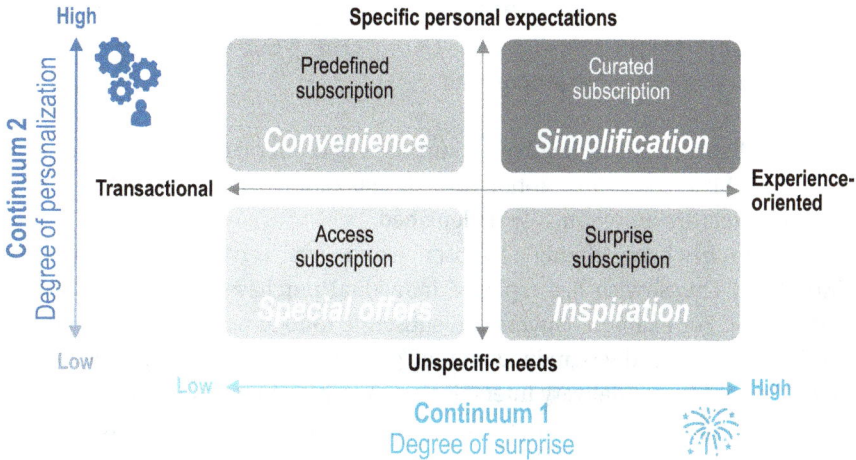

Figure 2.1: Typology of the four basic types of consumer goods subscriptions.
Source: Based on Bischof (2019)

subscriptions, curated subscriptions are personalized and require customers to be more open towards buying a variety of products. Ideally, the delivered products match individual preferences.

The surprise mechanism may lead to both positive and negative consumer experiences. Being inspired by new and surprising products, and thus expanding one's knowledge of a certain product category, is a positive feature of surprise subscriptions. The risk of receiving unattractive and unwanted products, on the other hand, has a fundamentally negative effect on the consumer experience. Especially if a curated subscription promises to deliver products that match individual preferences, disappointing deliveries may negatively impact the customer experience due to increased expectations. Surprise subscriptions therefore pose risk-related difficulties for both providers and consumers. Depending on whether consumers are able to check the delivered items in advance, and thus verify whether these items meet their individual preferences, subscriptions involve a different degree of uncertainty and risk for the consumer. The following sections discuss the four individual subscription types.

2.2 Predefined subscriptions

2.2.1 Definition and value proposition

Predefined subscriptions involve no surprises and offer customers self-selected products. This type of subscription provides maximum convenience: Frequently used products are automatically replenished.

Amazon has been offering a "Subscribe and Save" service in many countries since 2007. This service has replaced individual purchases (Berg and Knights, 2019, p. 95). For example, buyers can subscribe to food or household items, instead of buying products individually at great expense. Buyers can determine product quantity and delivery intervals (from monthly to semi-annual). In return, Amazon grants subscribers a discount of up to 15 percent on the selected articles (Berg and Knights, 2019, p. 95).

The American company Dollar Shave Club offers subscription razors and shaving heads. Blacksocks, a Swiss manufacturer of men's underwear and one of the oldest subscription providers, sells subscription socks and other fashion items. Customers determine both product quantity and delivery intervals. During the entire subscription period, the ordered products remain unchanged. Thus, consumers know exactly which products they will receive. Predefined subscriptions involve no risk and offer customers full transparency.

2.2.2 Purchase motives and consumer behavior

Predefined subscriptions aim to automate the regular purchase of certain products. These include, above all, products that do not play a very important emotional role in consumers' lives. The key motives for taking out such subscriptions are comfort and convenience. Predefined subscriptions therefore need to be positioned transactionally. They are in demand when consumers primarily require convenience in purchasing a certain product or product category.

This type of subscription can replace regular purchases. It is widespread in the US, where subscriptions are very popular. One of the main reasons for buying predefined subscriptions is regular demand. As many as 22 percent of consumers buying predefined subscriptions consider regular demand to be the main purchasing reason, compared to only 18 percent for curated, 13 percent for surprise, and 10 percent for access subscriptions. According to our survey, subscribers are highly apathetic toward product categories purchased via predefined subscriptions. They generally regard purchasing such products as burdensome.

2.3 Curated subscriptions

2.3.1 Definition and value proposition

The main benefit of curated subscriptions is reduced complexity. Curated subscriptions satisfy the desire for variety and personalization and aim to simplify purchasing decisions. This type of subscription is highly appreciated by consumers when they need purchasing assistance (provided in the form of individually curated product proposals). Product compilation results in a manageable surprise, especially as personal preferences are taken into account.

Suppliers such as Stitch Fix, Birchbox, Sephora Play!, and HelloFresh offer curated subscriptions for fashion, cosmetics, and food. They send out surprise boxes whose content is selected by the provider but tailored to individual subscriber preferences. Although the degree of personalization varies from provider to provider, box contents are adapted to individual preferences. Stitch Fix offers highly advanced personalization and assembles separate fashion packages for every customer. HelloFresh, on the other hand, sends out a limited number of menu boxes every week and makes customer-specific recommendations. Even though HelloFresh does not assemble its boxes individually, recommendations are nevertheless curated. All these providers endeavor to provide every customer with individual, personalized recommendations.

2.3.2 Purchase motives and consumer behavior

Consumers purchasing curated subscriptions are largely risk-averse and aim to simplify their purchasing search process. Other motives include variety seeking or timesaving. The surprise aspect, which is mitigated by curating, helps consumers to discover new products, thus adding to the appeal of this subscription type. At 39 percent, the motive to discover novelty is more pronounced with this type than with the other three types.

Curated subscriptions arouse a high level of interest but are not convincing. Curated subscription providers suffer the highest cancellation rates. Our study showed that 30 percent of consumers taking out curated subscriptions cancel within the first month (i.e., after the first delivery). This percentage greatly surpasses that for predefined (14 percent), surprise (20 percent), and access subscriptions (20 percent). A total of 21 percent of all subscribers cited unconvincing product selection as the main reason for terminating their subscription.

However, if a curated subscription meets a buyer's taste, it holds the greatest potential for customer retention. As many as 24 percent of the consumers we surveyed subscribed to a curated subscription for more than two years, a higher proportion than with predefined (17 percent), surprise (8 percent), and access subscriptions (5 percent). Despite these comparatively good figures, there is considerable potential for improving the range of services.

2.4 Surprise subscriptions

2.4.1 Definition and value proposition

Surprise subscriptions have a highly developed surprise mechanism. They satisfy experience-oriented needs and require great demand for product diversity, as they provide subscribers with new and unexpected products. Providers such as GLOSSYBOX, Try the World, and SprezzaBox, as well as curated subscriptions, deliver boxes with surprising product content. However, surprise subscriptions provide customers no control or prior knowledge of the specific products they will receive as part of the subscription prior to purchase. Surprise subscriptions are considered surprising because consumers have no say in item selection. Compared to curated subscriptions, consumers receive a selection of products that are not tailored to their individual preferences.

Surprise subscriptions and curated subscriptions both satisfy the need to be inspired by new products. Surprise subscriptions, however, are far riskier from a provider's perspective, as subscribers have no say in box composition. GLOS-SYBOX, a cosmetics surprise subscription, for example, sends all subscribers a monthly delivery containing the same products.

2.4.2 Purchase motives and consumer behavior

Surprise subscriptions offer variety, experience, and stimulation for novelty. But the thrill – of being surprised – and the risk – of receiving unwanted products – requires openness. The desire to try out new products or brands is a principal reason for purchasing surprise subscriptions. Asked about their main reason for buying a surprise subscription, 30 percent of respondents reported their desire to try out something new. Surprise purchases are emotional and hedonic and associated with pleasure.

Only 13 percent of respondents indicated regular product use as a primary motive for buying a surprise subscription, compared to 18 percent with curated subscriptions. Flexible termination is therefore considered six times more important with surprise subscriptions (13 percent) than with curated subscriptions (2 percent). For 22 percent of surprise subscribers, the main reason for cancellation is the desire to buy products only when these are actually needed. Surprise subscriptions are therefore not suited to meeting demand but focus on experiencing their surprise mechanism.

Buyers of surprise subscriptions strongly resemble adventure shoppers. They enjoy shopping in the respective product category, relish grappling with product innovations, and are generally interested in shopping, whether stationary or digitally. Adventure shoppers embrace risk and are unafraid of purchasing innovations. The almost complete absence of transactional buying motives means that surprise subscription providers are advised to send customers real surprises with outstanding novelty and to emphasize experience – the more exclusive the product range and presentation, the better.

2.5 Access subscriptions

2.5.1 Definition and value proposition

Access subscriptions, the fourth type, differ from the other three types. This type of subscription enables customers to purchase exclusive items. Such offerings exist as exclusive products and at reduced prices. As often happens with online newspapers, this range of products, which is geared to a specific need, is located behind a paywall and only available to subscribers.

Companies such as JustFab, Thrive Market, and Swarovski Crystal Society charge a fee for membership in their respective fashion, food, and decoration clubs. As with the Swarovski Crystal Society, these providers enable their members to purchase exclusive products that are unavailable in retail stores. Thrive Market offers its customers purely natural and organic food at reduced prices, while JustFab offers subscribers bargains on exclusive clothing items.

Access subscriptions appeal to consumers highly interested in limited offers. The principal purchasing motive is exclusive interest in a clearly defined product group. Access subscriptions channel the purchasing process such that subscribers will only find products that fit the supplier's needs. Customers purchase a guarantee against bad buys (i.e., purchases they regret having spent money on), because access subscription products are strictly aligned with the benefit promised by the subscription.

2.5.2 Purchase motives and consumer behavior

Access subscriptions focus on transactional goals. The main purchase reasons are price advantages and a special product selection. Beyond their financial benefits, access subscriptions also offer curated product ranges that cater to a niche (see, for instance, JustFab and Thrive Market for new fashion or organic food). This facilitates decision making in consumers: They are sure that the subscription provides a product range that is more appropriate to their niche compared to stationary stores' offerings. Thus, the overarching value proposition of access subscriptions is that they simplify buying by offering a coherent assortment.

The surveyed German-Swiss buyers of access subscriptions are pioneers: They have clear ideas about the respective product category and uncompromisingly pursue these interests. Accordingly, such subscribers are so-called *mavens* and express their expertise within their sphere of influence. Access subscriptions are therefore well suited to clear-cut niche positioning in order to account for this consumer group's pioneering spirit.

The idea of charging a subscription fee to purchase exclusive products has not yet established itself in German-speaking Switzerland. This subscription type is strongly underrepresented in our sample (only two companies). Only about 4 percent of German-speaking Swiss have an access subscription. Attractive offers are needed to improve the low retention rate. This subscription type has a low customer retention rate of 25 percent. The main reasons for cancellation are poor product ranges and poor product quality. Access providers should place special emphasis on offering convincing exclusive offers.

2.6 Examples of subscription providers

Table 2.1 shows the variety of subscriptions currently available on the market. We present four or five international subscription providers in three product categories: Fashion and Clothing, Food and Cooking, and Cosmetics and Decoration. These represent the individual subscription types. The columns "Surprise" and "Personalization" refer to the two dimensions of our typology in terms of the degree of surprise and personalization, and thus define subscription type.

Table 2.1 also shows that every subscription type exists in several product categories. Further, subscription prices vary significantly. The average price of Stitch

Table 2.1: Selected subscription providers and their trading mechanisms.

Product category	Company	Price	Number of articles per delivery	Delivery interval	Return possible	Surprise Experience orientation > transactionality	Personalization Low tolerance necessary for product variety	Subscription type
Fashion and Clothing	**Blacksocks** *blacksocks.com*	Approx. $10–$20 per pair	Selectable (min. 3 pairs)	Selectable (e.g., quarterly)	No	No	Yes (product selection)	**Predefined**
	Stitch Fix * *Stitchfix.com*	Approx. $275 per box	5 articles	Selectable (e.g., monthly)	Yes	Yes	Yes	**Curated**
	JustFab *Justfab.com*	$39.95 monthly	Selectable	Selectable (consumption-dependent)	Yes	No	No	**Access**
	SprezzaBox *Sprezzabox.com*	Approx. $25 per box	5 to 6	Once a month	No	Yes	No	**Surprise**

(continued)

Table 2.1 (continued)

Product category	Company	Price	Number of articles per delivery	Delivery interval	Return possible	Surprise Experience orientation > transactionality	Personalization Low tolerance necessary for product variety	Subscription type
Food and Cooking	**Amazon Subscribe and Save** *Amazon.com*	Depends on the product	Selectable	Selectable (e.g., monthly, half-yearly)	No	No	Yes (product selection)	Predefined
	HelloFresh *Hellofresh.com*	Approx. $50 – $125 per box (US)	Selectable (Recipes for 2–4 persons)	Once a week	No	Yes	Conditional (recommendation)	Curated
	Thrive Market * *Thrivemarket.com*	$59.95 per annum	Selectable (consumption-dependent)	Selectable (consumption-dependent)	No	No	No	Access
	Try the World * *Trytheworld.com*	Approx. $29 – $39 per box	5 to 10	Once a month	No	Yes	No	Surprise

				Selectable (e.g., bi-monthly, quarterly)		Yes (product selection)	Predefined
Cosmetics and Decoration	**Dollar Shave Club** * *Dollarshaveclub.com*	$25 per box	2 articles (or more)	No	No	No	
	Birchbox * *birchbox.com*	Approx. $15 per box	5 articles (sample only)	Once a month	Yes	Partly (curated and non-curated options)	**Curated**
	Sephora Play! * *Sephora.com*	$10	5 articles (sample only)	Once a month	Yes	Partial (different boxes)	**Curated**
	Swarovski Crystal Society *Swarovski.com*	$49	>1 figure per year	Yearly	Conditional (Collect)	No	**Access**
	GLOSSYBOX *Glossybox.com*	Approx. $20	5 articles	Once a month	Yes	No	**Surprise**

Suppliers marked with "*" are currently unavailable in the DACH (D ("Germany"), A ("Austria"), and CH ("Switzerland")) region.
Source: Based on Bischof, Boettger, and Rudolph (2019). Status: December 2019

Fix, a curated fashion subscription, is $275 per shipment compared to $30–60 for a quarterly Blacksocks socks subscription.

Subscription types differ considerably in terms of delivery cycles, delivery intervals, and return options. There are no limits to entrepreneurial creativity in designing subscriptions. We hope that interested retailers will find the following list inspiring.

3 Customer behavior and subscription types

3.1 Research design of our consumer survey

The following results are taken from our representative 2018 market survey of 568 Swiss consumers. Survey participants came from Switzerland and represent the local population in terms of income, age, and gender. They were recruited via an online panel of a recognized market research company (Rudolph, Bischof, and Schuerch, 2019).

We asked participants about their familiarity with 54 subscription providers (identified among 224 providers operating in German-speaking Europe). We abstracted their relevance based on various factors (e.g., number of visitors to provider websites). Respondents rated their familiarity with every provider. Depending on their familiarity, consumers indicated whether they were interested in these subscription providers, why they cancelled their subscription, or why they continued subscribing. The answers provided valuable insights into consumer behavior by subscription type.

3.2 Interest in subscriptions and conversion rates

Subscription sales are still low among the most popular subscription providers in Switzerland. Overall, consumers are only moderately interested in subscriptions. For example, of the 568 consumers surveyed, only 112 and 136 respectively were interested in the five most popular providers of predefined or surprise subscriptions (see Figure 3.1). Comparatively, curated subscriptions fared better, with around twice as many (i.e., 263) consumers being generally interested in the five largest curated subscriptions. Access subscriptions lagged far behind the other subscription types, partly due to their low penetration in the German-speaking world. Of the 568 respondents, only 45 consumers were interested in the two largest providers, due to a lack of alternatives.

However, calculating their conversion rate, and thus the proportion of interested consumers relative to the resulting subscribers, shows that many providers could very well enjoy entrepreneurial success as the market matures. To calculate the conversion rate, we refer to the five most important providers per subscription type. Access subscriptions are currently not widespread in the consumer goods sector (thus only two providers could be considered). Concentrating on the five largest subscriptions prevents distortions and provides an objective basis for comparing subscription types. The fragmented subscription market makes it necessary

https://doi.org/10.1515/9783110730197-003

Of **568** survey respondents …

...**112**	...**263**	...**136**	...**45**
were interested in the Top 5[1]	were interested in the Top 5[1]	were interested in the Top 5[1]	were interested in the Top 2[1]
Predefined subscriptions	Curated subscriptions	Surprise subscriptions	Access subscriptions
Of which ... *Conversion rate* 14%	Of which ... *Conversion rate* 25%	Of which ... *Conversion rate* 24%	Of which ... *Conversion rate* 9%
...**16**	...**67**	...**32**	...**4**
had a Predefined subscription	had a Curated subscription	had a Surprise subscription	had an Access subscription

Details

> We calculated the conversion rate by considering the **five most important providers of the four subscription types** (only two providers offered Access subscriptions)

> **The conversion rate varies greatly. It is highest for Curated (25%) and Surprise (24%) subscriptions**

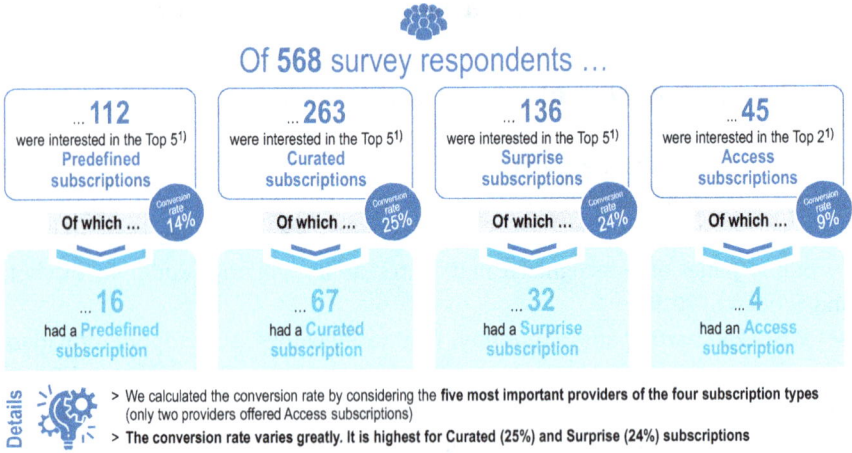

1) The Top-5 most purchased subscriptions per subscription type: **Predefined:** Blacksocks, Sox in a Box, Dein Kaffee, Pets Premium, Mornin' Glory; **Curated:** Mondovino, Outfittery, Zalon, HelloFresh, Kukimi; **Surprise:** Pink Box, Früchtebox-Express, Marley Spoon, Lidl Menübox, Glossybox; **Access:** Swarovski Crystal Society, Myonbelle (only two providers)

Figure 3.1: Conversion rates by subscription type.
Source: Rudolph, Bischof, and Schürch (2019)

to concentrate on the most important subscriptions: Although 18 percent of respondents had an active subscription at the time of survey, they were distributed among many small suppliers, whose conversion rates were not representative due to their relative unfamiliarity.

Conversion rates vary greatly. Of those consumers who were interested in a subscription offer, 25 percent purchased a curated subscription, 24 percent a surprise subscription, 14 percent a predefined subscription, and 9 percent an access subscription. The conversion rate for curated subscription providers is therefore almost twice as high as for predefined subscriptions. Specifically, 263 out of our 568 respondents were interested in a curated subscription. Of these, 67 had a curated subscription. The low number of customers per provider can be attributed to the still young market.

3.3 Significance of subscriptions by product groups

Subscriptions have not yet established themselves on the market. Hence, it is advisable to investigate customer behavior in an exploratory way. In order to establish the significance of subscriptions for individual categories, we asked respondents to rate highly popular product categories. Respondents expressed their agreement with subscription attractiveness in the respective product category on a 7-point scale. A higher rating corresponds to a higher acceptance of subscriptions in the respective category (see Figure 3.2).

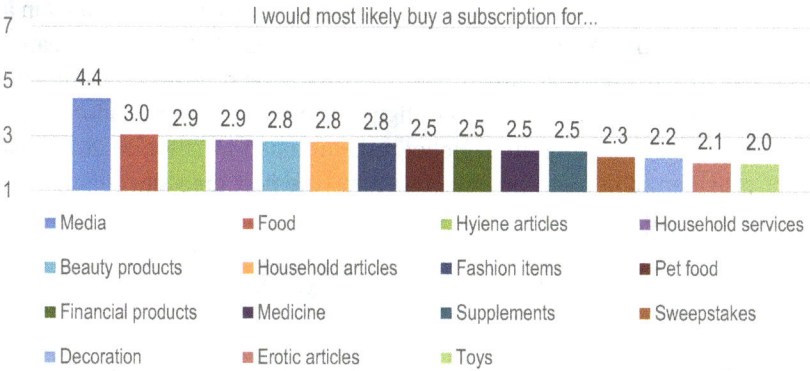

I would most likely buy a subscription for...

7

5   4.4

3   3.0   2.9   2.9   2.8   2.8   2.8   2.5   2.5   2.5   2.5   2.3   2.2   2.1   2.0

1

■ Media   ■ Food   ■ Hyiene articles   ■ Household services

■ Beauty products   ■ Household articles ■ Fashion items   ■ Pet food

■ Financial products ■ Medicine   ■ Supplements   ■ Sweepstakes

■ Decoration   ■ Erotic articles   ■ Toys

Figure 3.2: Acceptance of subscriptions per product category.
Legend: 7 = "Agree completely"; 1 = "Do not agree at all"
Source: Rudolph, Bischof, and Schürch (2019)

Media subscriptions (e.g., Amazon Prime, Netflix) seem to be well suited to automation and are considered by consumers to be the most relevant subscription category. In the consumer goods sector, however, consumers are currently most likely to automate their purchases of food and hygiene products. Subscriptions for toys, erotic, and decorative goods are the least popular. Categories with many subscription providers (food) perform better than categories with few providers (toys).

Physical consumer goods are currently less likely to be purchased via subscriptions. Average purchase probability for most physical consumer goods is far below the mean rating ("4") on the 7-point scale. The number of currently sold subscriptions is rather low among the examined subscription providers, which may be related to the novelty of subscriptions. This becomes particularly clear when looking at the wide distribution of subscriptions in the media sector (where subscriptions are already well-established). Accordingly, due to the proliferation of media subscriptions, consumers' inclinations to consume media via subscriptions are much higher than in physical product categories.

3.4 Preferred subscription types by product groups

Although subscriptions are as yet unable to convince the majority of people, interest is increasing. Well-known companies with strong brands can quickly gain market share in the subscription market. However, they should have the necessary perseverance to establish their subscription offers in what remains a young market. This market is still highly fragmented: It has many small suppliers, most of which are independent start-ups and managed by established dealers only in a few cases. Thus, within a year of its launch in August 2017, Lidl Menübox soared into the top 10 most popular subscriptions in Switzerland. However, Lidl cancelled this offering in early 2019 as sales figures did not meet expectations. One example of patience paying off is HelloFresh (founded in 2011). In 2019, the meal-kit provider achieved a positive result for the first time since its IPO in 2017 (Reuters, 2020).

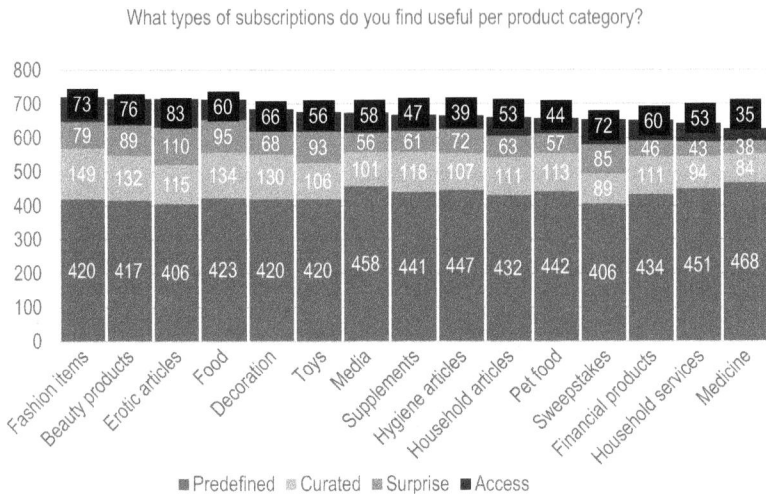

What types of subscriptions do you find useful per product category?

■ Predefined ▧ Curated ■ Surprise ■ Access

Figure 3.3: Preferred subscription types by product groups.
Source: Rudolph, Bischof, and Schürch (2019)

No subscription is like another. This truism makes it opportune to inquire which subscription type best fits which product category. We asked our survey respondents to report their preferred subscription type (or types) per product group; multiple choices were possible if respondents found that several subscription types for a product group made sense. In terms of the number of entries, consumers rated predefined subscriptions as the most useful subscription type across categories (see Figure 3.3). This type achieved a remarkable 82 percent approval rate for medical products (468 out of 568 possible mentions). A total of 26 percent of respondents found curated subscriptions best suited for fashion and clothing purchases while 34 percent approved of surprise subscriptions for erotic products. In the future, retail subscriptions will therefore offer further potential.

3.5 Customer retention

Once prospects have been converted to customers and been persuaded to buy, the second challenge of a subscription service becomes apparent: to retain customers for the long term. A subscription service tailored to customer needs offers companies the opportunity to build stable and profitable customer relationships. However, subscription providers suffer from high churn rates. A subscription's customer retention rate (i.e., the proportion of currently active subscribers among all previous subscribers) is one of its key performance indicators (KPIs). This rate determines subscription success and indicates how well providers meet customer needs. Only a few providers have managed to position themselves as service providers with excellent service offerings and thus to achieve high customer retention.

To calculate customer retention rates, we used the same questions about consumers' familiarity with subscription providers that we used to calculate conversion rates. Here, however, we considered information on all 54 subscriptions, as even small providers can provide compelling subscription experiences. We calculated the customer retention rate as the share of current subscribers relative to all subscriptions (including cancelled subscriptions) (see Figure 3.4). In total, 167 out of 568 respondents already had a subscription. In 103 cases, the subscription was still active in May 2018. Of course, these consumers may also have bought more than one subscription (as shown in Figure 3.4).

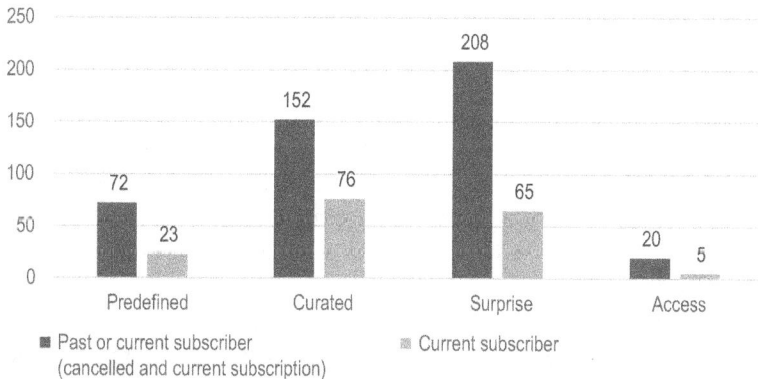

Figure 3.4: Customer retention rates by subscription type.
Source: Rudolph, Bischof, and Schürch (2019)

Comparing customer retention rates among subscription types reveals clear differences in the ability of providers to build and maintain long-term customer loyalty. On average, providers retained only 52 percent (Curated), 32 percent

(Predefined), 31 percent (Surprise), and 25 percent (Access) of their existing customers. Thus, the customer retention rate is highest for curated subscriptions (lowest cancellation rate). The curation mechanism of curated subscriptions seems to be superior to the predefined subscriptions approach, which involves no surprises whatsoever.

On average, subscriptions including a predefinition or surprise mechanism only retained 32 percent of their customers on average. Curated subscription boxes (i.e., products are adapted to individual preferences) seem to be more promising (52 percent). Although 24 percent of curated subscribers reported that they subscribed for at least 24 months, 30 percent dropped out after just one month (i.e., after the first delivery). Hence, only truly tailored subscriptions enable companies to build stable and profitable customer relationships (see Figure 3.5).

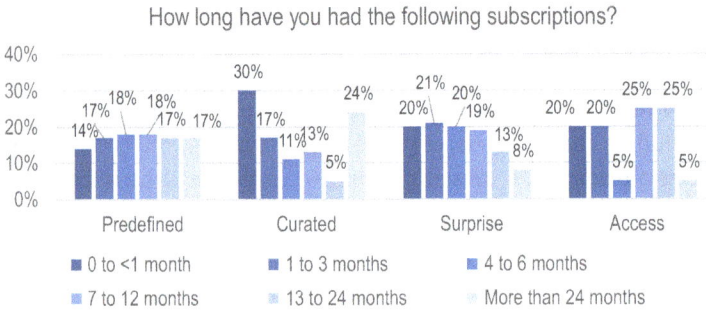

Figure 3.5: Subscription duration by subscription type.
Source: Rudolph, Bischof, and Schürch (2019)

Curated subscriptions are a double-edged sword: They work well for one customer but badly for another. While 24 percent of curated subscribers indicated a subscription length of at least 24 months, 30 percent dropped out after just one month. Curated subscriptions persuade many consumers to make a first purchase by promising specific benefits: individual personalization and highly discounted initial deliveries (e.g., HelloFresh). Yet their value proposition also leads to inflated expectations: Customers cancel more quickly if they are dissatisfied. At the same time, however, the high proportion of long-term subscribers to curated subscriptions testifies to high customer value once a customer's taste has been hit.

3.6 Improving retention

Subscription service providers must create an excellent customer experience, one that enables convenient automation of consumption. In the following paragraphs, we present the main reasons for cancellation by subscription type (as identified in our quantitative study). This overview provides managers with a more differentiated perspective on customer retention. Many subscription service providers need to improve their operations and focus more on customer behavior and benefits.

Predefined subscriptions should provide flexibility regarding delivery quantities and intervals. The main cancellation reason cited by 22 percent of consumers cancelling their predefined subscription was their inability to consume the delivered products quickly enough. Effective ways of improving customer retention include being able to adjust timing, quantity, and intervals to personal needs, as well as being able to pause or skip deliveries.

Curated subscriptions must offer a convincing range of products. Poorly satisfied customer expectations are the main reason for terminating a curated subscription. Customer knowledge, especially of preferences, habits and priorities, as well as subsequent appropriate product selection, are part of the value proposition of curated subscriptions. If subscribers remain customers for a longer time, providers learn more about customer preferences and thus can ensure better curated offerings. OUTFITTERY, for example, sells tailored clothing and thus learns more about its customers with every delivery cycle. Using machine learning algorithms can help to better match the recommended products with subscribers.

Surprise subscriptions are better received if customers can choose delivery intervals. Contrary to predefined and curated subscriptions, the decisive reason for cancellation is neither product quantity nor product selection but the desire to buy a product only when it is needed. This creates a dilemma for many surprise subscribers. On the one hand, they want surprises, but on the other they do not need many of these products. Providers must solve this dilemma in order to lower the cancellation rate – if necessary by offering greater flexibility with quantity and interval selection, as with predefined subscriptions.

Access subscriptions become more attractive with increasing transparency regarding the range of products offered. Poor assortment and poor product quality are the principal reasons for cancelling access subscriptions. For instance, subscribers to the Swarovski Crystal Society do not know before paying their subscription fee which glass figurines will be available for purchase during the subscription period. Similarly, MyOnbelle subscribers do not know which dresses will be available. Greater transparency about product ranges increases consumers' pre-purchase knowledge, hence attracting more customers to whom the range is suited. This may positively impact customer retention. Conversely, increased assortment transparency means that more customers will not purchase a subscription if an assortment fails to meet their needs.

3.7 Demographic characteristics of subscribers

Subscriptions have yet to establish themselves in everyday life. It is therefore worth considering the demographic characteristics of subscribers (see Figure 3.6). The novelty of subscriptions in retail makes it reasonable to assume that the probability of a subscription purchase depends in particular on socio-demographic aspects. In the following paragraphs, we discuss which customer segments are particularly well suited to subscriptions and thus can be attracted to such offers.

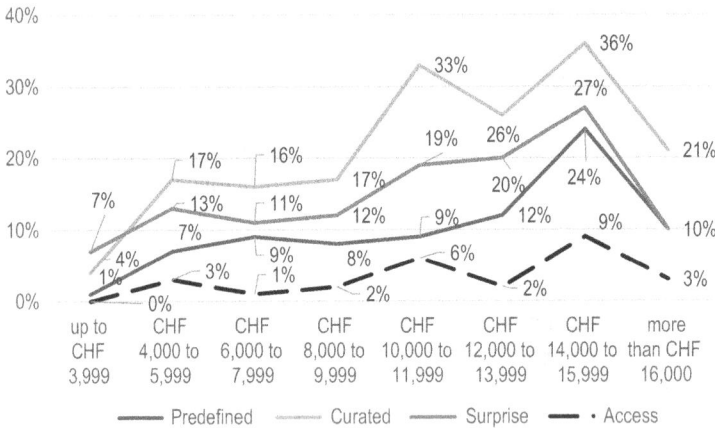

Figure 3.6: Share of subscribers by income class.
Source: Rudolph, Bischof, and Schürch (2019)
N = 568

Subscribers have an above-average gross household income. A total of 36 percent of consumers with a monthly gross household income of CHF 14, 000–15,999 have already purchased a curated subscription. Regular subscription deliveries mean that consumers might receive products even if they do not need them. Subscriptions therefore quickly increase consumption beyond what is necessary and are therefore unattractive for lower income groups.

Subscribers are often younger people (see Figure 3.7). Young professionals (25–34 years) are a suitable target group for subscriptions. Actual subscription usage is by far highest in this group, especially for curated and surprise

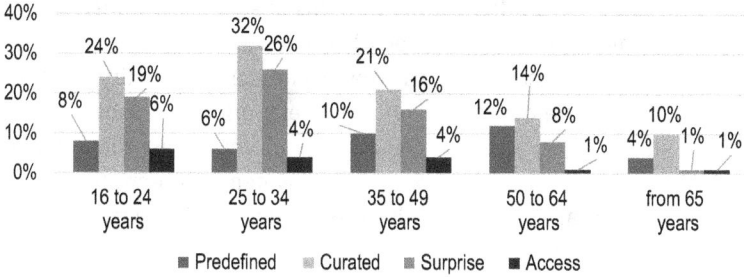

Figure 3.7: Share of subscribers by age group.
Source: Rudolph, Bischof, and Schürch (2019)
N = 568

subscriptions. A total of 32 percent and 26 percent of consumers aged 25 to 34 years have already purchased a curated or surprise subscription at some point, compared to only 10 percent and 1 percent of consumers more than 65 years of age. Surprise subscriptions are therefore better suited to younger target groups.

Although subscription use declines with increasing age, certain types of subscriptions are especially well-suited to older consumers. The share of consumers buying predefined subscriptions is highest among consumers aged 50 to 64 years (12 percent). The convenience aspect of consumer automation therefore appears to be a priority for older customers. This type of subscription can be particularly useful for them (due to reduced mobility at a higher age). Access subscriptions are not very popular across all segments (1 percent – 6 percent).

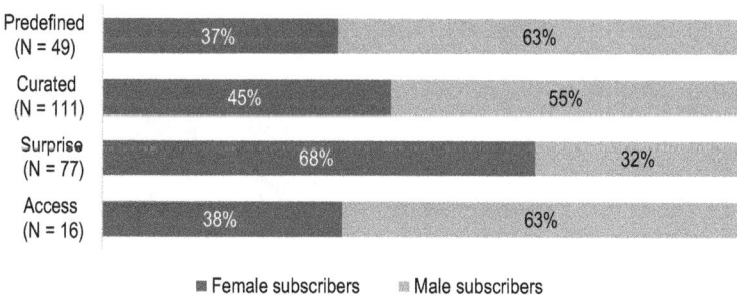

Figure 3.8: Share of subscribers by gender and subscription type.
Source: Rudolph, Bischof, and Schürch (2019)
N = 568

Gender also seems to be a differentiator in terms of subscription preferences (see Figure 3.8). Female buyers tend to prefer hedonic subscriptions with a surprise factor (e.g., surprise subscription) and appreciate the opportunity to be inspired by subscriptions. Male buyers, in contrast, prefer utilitarian subscriptions (e.g., predefined subscription) and therefore, above all, appreciate the automation aspect, which routinizes the purchase of everyday items. Subscriptions with additional benefits such as individual advice (e.g., curated subscription) are equally popular with both genders.

4 Recommendations for developing subscription services

This chapter discusses how to implement a subscription-based business idea and presents initial recommendations for action. The findings are based on qualitative interviews with managers of well-known subscription providers (Rudolph, Bischof, Boettger, and Weiler, 2017). We interviewed managers from various subscription companies (food, fashion, and cosmetics). These companies use subscriptions as their basic business model rather than as a means of merely complementing traditional retail activities. Hence, our proposals build on intensive learning.

Our recommendations rest on fundamental insights into subscription revenue mechanisms. The key question is: Which revenue sources and approaches seem to be appropriate for our four subscription types? Next, we present a step-by-step concept for establishing successful subscriptions. Our suggestions provide food for thought that companies will need to amend as they see fit.

4.1 Revenue mechanisms and KPIs for different subscription types

In this book, we limit ourselves to a few, yet important suggestions. The demand for new subscription revenue models strikes us as crucial. Any attempt to establish profitable subscriptions based on the "margin logic" of classical retailers will soon fail. Although all subscription types aim to generate recurring purchases, the four subscription types presented here differ fundamentally in terms of revenue mechanisms (see Table 4.1).

4.1.1 Main revenue sources

Predefined and surprise subscriptions have a long-term profitability perspective and pay for themselves over a subscriber's lifetime due to their high degree of automation. For example, the Blacksocks socks subscription is prepared to invest the first-year contribution margin to acquire new customers, and thus focuses on the long-term profitability of customer relationships: "Subscription renewal after the first delivery is the critical moment. If customers continue their subscription after the first delivery, they remain customers as long as blood flows through their legs" (S. Liechti, interview in Rudolph, Bischof, Boettger, and

https://doi.org/10.1515/9783110730197-004

Weiler, 2017). Surprise subscriptions also achieve scaling effects, since all customers receive the same products. Also, adding further customers has no significant impact on the subscription's cost structure. The two aforementioned subscription types (Predefined and Surprise) therefore attempt to establish long-term customer relationships.

Situated at the interface between convenience and inspiration, curated subscriptions generate revenue through personalization services. Sometimes very high, the costs incurred should be covered in the short term. Unlike surprise subscriptions, curated subscriptions have seldom relied on sources of income other than membership fees and revenues from product sales (see Section 4.1.2). Only if personalization can be automated in the long run using historical data, and if more accurate recommendations result from data analysis, does a long-term revenue perspective make sense. However, since curated subscriptions (e.g., OUTFITTERY) are largely personalized by humans (e.g., initial telephone interviews, regular discussions with customers), every order should be profitable on its own.

Access subscriptions aim to sell their customers the largest possible shopping baskets. However, since product ranges change regularly and are not personalized on an individual customer basis, the shopping experience resembles that of an online shop. Subscriptions do not automatically lead to purchases in the case of access subscriptions. As the example of the Swarovski Crystal Society shows, customers must actively select glass figures from an exclusive range. Subscribing to the Swarovski Crystal Society only entitles customers to purchase the exclusive product range. Besides the annual membership fee, no further sales are automatically generated. Rather, this very much depends on the exclusive product range. Unless they perceive this as attractive, subscribers cancel their subscription after a short time. This risk means that access subscriptions should pay for themselves already in the first year.

4.1.2 Additional revenue sources

In order to cope with the sometimes-high costs of acquiring new customers, the providers of predefined and surprise subscriptions are advised to develop additional revenue sources. This can be achieved, for example, through an online shop. Blacksocks operates an online shop that generates 50 percent of sales. Mornin' Glory, a German razor blade subscription service, intends to add further products in the future (e.g., intimate care products). As one expert puts it: "Subscriptions are a starting point for expanding into other related niche categories" (F. Paltenghi, interview in Rudolph, Bischof, Boettger, and Weiler, 2017). Finally, the possibility of cross-selling motivated Unilever to purchase the Dollar Shave Club for more than $1 billion, "as few of these companies are successful in the long term by selling a single product" (Livsey, 2017).

Surprise subscriptions generate additional income through market research-related cooperation with consumer goods producers. Surprise subscriptions are interesting for producers because the surprise mechanism attracts consumers with a particularly high affinity for the respective product category. Surprise subscription providers can use customer surveys not only to obtain their subscribers' opinions on the surprise products but also to sell the results to producers. The managing director of GLOSSYBOX, the international cosmetics subscription, underlines the positioning of surprise subscriptions as a marketing channel for manufacturers and differentiates such subscriptions from regular retailers. This difference manifests in a smaller product range and fast stock turnover: "The just-in-time production of surprise boxes and the different flows of goods differentiate us strongly from regular cosmetics retailers. I am competing with other communication channels like influencers" (C. Genthner-Kappesz, interview in Rudolph, Bischof, Boettger, and Weiler, 2017).

It is highly attractive for consumer goods manufacturers to present themselves to consumers with a high category affinity within the framework of a surprise subscription. This, moreover, gives subscription providers additional negotiating power when purchasing goods. They can fill their surprise boxes with seemingly inexpensive products as opposed to regular purchases. Further, they can charge the producer a fee for placing information or brochures. This requires good supplier management: "Independence from suppliers is very important for surprise subscriptions to work in the long term. You have to be careful not to regularly include the same products or brands in order to maintain consumer curiosity" (A. Grassler, interview in Rudolph, Bischof, Boettger, and Weiler, 2017).

4.1.3 KPIs

Winning customers is one thing but retaining them is another. Subscription providers concentrate their business activities on a few selected KPIs. These may differ among the four subscription types. Most of the interviewed companies work with three KPIs: customer acquisition costs, customer retention rate, and customer lifetime value (CLV). The latter two KPIs emphasize the goal of retaining customers over the long term.

One illustrative example is the Swarovski Crystal Society. Its average subscription period is approximately five years. In contrast, GLOSSYBOX or Glambox customers only remain with the company for half a year. Thus, customer numbers and especially retention rates considerably impact profitability (Gupta, Lehmann, and Stuart, 2004). The Swarovski Crystal Society achieves high customer lifetime value (CLV) through attractive product ranges and the resulting long subscription periods. The annual subscription fee (EUR 34) assumes a high basic interest in decorative glass figures. As Managing Director Ann-Sophie Mayr puts it: "The SCS serves a niche of around 150,000 members, all of whom are valuable consumers with a high CLV and have the highest annual expenditure of any Swarovski customer" (A. Mayr, interview in Rudolph, Bischof, Boettger, and Weiler, 2017).

Subscriptions with a strong retail component (e.g., an e-commerce shop) should also consider retail-related KPIs (e.g., average revenue per customer). Service-intensive curated subscriptions benefit from measuring their Net Promoter Score (i.e., the intention to recommend), while surprise subscriptions should aim to increase their reach to demonstrate their relevance as a marketing channel to manufacturers.

To reduce customer churn, subscription managers also aim to build a community in which subscribers can network and interact with like-minded people. This is especially worthwhile with surprise and access subscriptions, which attract consumers with a high affinity for the respective product category. It therefore makes sense to measure consumer engagement within the community, for example, by the number of likes or posts per subscriber, and to actively expand this indicator. GLOSSYBOX even transfers the community idea to the analog world and runs a beauty conference called Glossycon: "Our long-term goal is to create a world around the category of beauty products" (C. Genthner-Kappesz, interview, April 18, 2017 in Rudolph, Bischof, Boettger, and Weiler, 2017).

4.2 Step-by-step concept for establishing a subscription service

Based on our qualitative interviews and findings, we present a step-by-step concept to support managers in creating a subscription service. Figure 4.1 describes six steps that should ideally be considered. They involve selecting products and services, identifying potential customer segments, and defining key targets. We also discuss which subscription type is right for which purpose.

Table 4.1: Revenue mechanisms by subscription type.

		Predefined subscription	Curated subscription	Surprise subscription	Access subscription
Customer benefits	**Unique selling point (USP)**	– Comfort	– Personalization	– Inspiration	– Unique products
	Surprise	– Lower	– Medium	– Higher	– Higher
	Result	– Replenishment of selected products	– Controlled inspiration	– Inspiration by unexpected products	– Access
Revenue mechanisms	**Revenue perspective**	– Long-term profitability (high acquisition costs)	– Short- or long-term profitability	– Long-term profitability (establishing outreach)	– Short-term profitability (online shop)
	Critical aspects of success	– Long-term subscriber retention	– Cost efficiency of personalization service	– Scaling: acquiring subscribers and suppliers	– Developing a unique assortment
	Additional sources of revenue	– Online shop	– Membership fee	– Market research for manufacturers – Manufacturer pays for product placement in box – Online shop	– Membership fee – Online shop – Partial re-use of products (sharing of clothing)
	Assortment procurement	– Mainly own production	– Own production and third-party producers	– Mainly third-party manufacturers	– Own production and third-party producers – Niche curated products

(continued)

Table 4.1 (continued)

		Predefined subscription	Curated subscription	Surprise subscription	Access subscription
KPIs	**General KPIs** *General level*	– Box profit (profit per delivery) – Growth (of the customer base)			
	General KPIs *Customer level*	– Customer acquisition costs (costs for advertising and discounts) – Customer retention rate (probability of subscription continuance) – Customer lifetime value (expected contribution margin over lifetime)			
	Subscription-specific KPIs	– Cross-sales (online shop)	– Net Promoter Score – Average shopping cart size	– Cross-sales (online shop) – Engagement (community) – Producer profits (consumer survey)	– Cross-sales (online shop) – Membership duration – Exercised exclusivity
	Example company	– Blacksocks – Amazon Subscribe and Save – Dollar Shave Club	– Stitch Fix – HelloFresh – Birchbox/Sephora Play!	– SprezzaBox – Try the World – GLOSSYBOX	– Swarovski Crystal Society – JustFab – Thrive Market

Source: Our figure based on Bischof (2019)

1 Select product category	**2** Define customer segment	**3** Define key goals	**4** Select subscription archetype	**5** Add revenue sources	**6** Check for success
> Identify product categories with a competitive advantage > Prioritize strategically important categories > Decide which product category should be developed into a subscription	> Identify main customer segments within the selected product category > Analyze customer segments in terms of utilitarian (transactional) and hedonic (experience-oriented) needs	> Identify strengths and weaknesses in one's product range and decide on a subscription strategy: – Satisfying utilitarian needs through comfort – Satisfying hedonic needs through inspiration	> Increase convenience ***Predefined*** > Reduce purchasing complexity or increase personalization ***Curated Surprise*** > Inspire customers ***General Surprise*** > Offer unique products or prices ***Access***	> Cross-sell via online shop, etc. ***Predefined General Surprise Access*** > Sell product placements and customer reviews to producers ***Curated Surprise General Surprise*** > Organize community events ***Curated Surprise General Surprise Access***	**General KPIs** > General Level – Margin per box – Growth Rate > Customer Level – Churn rate – Customer lifetime value – Acquisition costs **Type-Specific KPIs** > Cross-sales via online shop > Added revenue: – Placements – Insights > Events

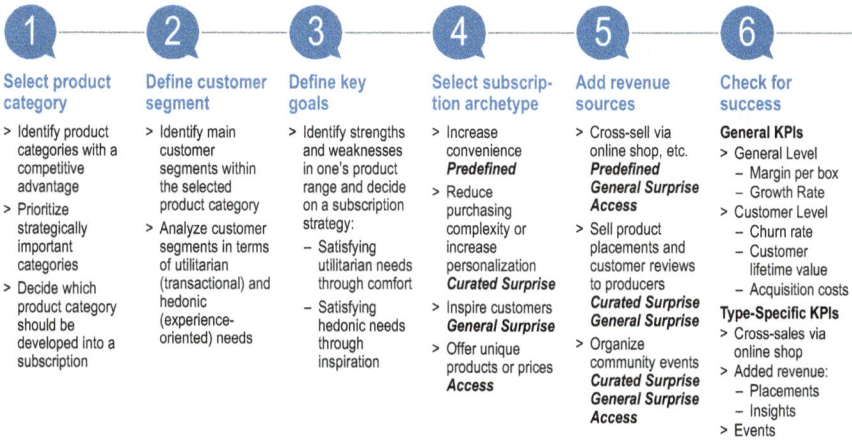

Figure 4.1: Step-by-step concept for establishing a subscription service.
Source: Based on Bischof (2019)

4.2.1 Select product category

First, select a product category that is suited to a subscription service. Suitable product categories include ones in which a provider is particularly popular and possesses a high level of expertise. A strong market position considerably helps providers because customers already trust the brand and the offerings. Marketing expenditure is lower for established brands. A surprise subscription introduced by an established cosmetics retailer would enjoy a level of trust that start-ups would need to gain first.

It is therefore feasible for established retailers to check their own expertise and to prioritize a product category accordingly. Existing consumer trust helps well-known brands to automate future purchases. The novelty of the subscription mechanism can enhance customer attention. Thus, when a subscription is introduced not only the service itself, but also the selected product category contributes to enhancing established dealers' brand value. However, well-known brands fear channel conflicts. No established supplier ranks among the 10 most popular providers of predefined subscriptions. Stationary retailers fear that automated delivery will diminish frequencies in their stationary branches.

New providers should carefully examine the competition for subscriptions and consider possible cooperations with other partners. This may help to avoid excessive initial investment.

Overall, provider expertise should therefore guide subscription orientation. It is advisable to focus a subscription on a few product groups or product categories with high brand awareness in order to make a convincing performance promise. While surprise or access subscriptions can also serve several product categories, these must follow a convincing value proposition.

4.2.2 Define customer segments

Second, target groups must be identified that are particularly interested in the selected product categories. Subscribers are often experts in the respective product category. A highly involved target group must overcome fewer obstacles to test a new concept and to purchase the product by subscription in the future.

Relevant target group(s) must be selected based on detailed analyses of consumer needs. The utilitarian and hedonic needs of the selected customer segment are crucial to the subsequent steps in establishing a subscription service (e.g., selection of subscription type). According to our subscription typology, we recommend analyzing the transactional and experience-oriented needs of all potentially relevant target groups. Thus, for instance, is the target segment more interested in simplifying its shopping than emotionalizing it? Focus group interviews with so-called "lead users" help to determine how to expand a product subscription with interesting services. This knowledge is highly important for the sixth step: profitability.

4.2.3 Define key goals

The third level involves comparing the identified target group's needs with the provider's strengths. This enables providers to better decide whether they should introduce a subscription to strengthen an existing strength or close a gap in their service offering. Regarding consumer needs, we distinguish between utilitarian (i.e., functional and transactional) and hedonic (i.e., experience-oriented and emotional) needs. A subscription provider can respond to consumers' utilitarian needs by offering subscriptions that simplify and automate purchase decisions, while satisfying hedonic needs by inspiring consumers with new ideas and products.

It is probably more cost-effective if existing providers introduce subscriptions that build on their strengths and expertise. Opposing positioning alternatives, which turn existing weaknesses into strengths, encounter cognitive dissonance. Discounters, for example, would be better advised to introduce transactional rather than experience-based subscriptions, as their limited product range is geared toward an efficient and uninspiring shopping experience. Department stores, on the other hand, would be better advised to introduce experience-oriented and thus surprising subscriptions, since their limited assortment is primarily aimed at experience-oriented consumers.

4.2.4 Select subscription type

Fourth, select one of two subscription types. Experience-oriented subscriptions (e.g., curated and surprise) offer a hedonic customer experience through surprises. Such subscriptions can attract consumers to new ideas and products, as well as satisfy inspirational curiosity. Curated subscriptions further reduce complexity and search effort by suggesting preferred products.

Predefined and access subscriptions, on the other hand, automate purchase decisions and primarily satisfy basic utilitarian needs. A predefined subscription automates repeat purchases, while access subscriptions for organic food (e.g., Thrive Market) offer an exclusive range of products in the most convenient way. Their buyers appreciate convenient shopping, also because such subscriptions significantly reduce search efforts. Access subscription products might be offered at lower prices because prepaid membership fees and regular purchases facilitate business planning.

4.2.5 Add revenue sources

Fifth, subscription profitability can be increased by charging for additional services. For example, monthly membership fees and additional sales via online shops can increase profitability. Another viable option is to charge consumer goods companies for featuring their products in a subscription box. The same applies to the provider's consultancy, subscriber feedback, and many other services (Rudolph, Bischof, Boettger, and Weiler, 2017). Subscription profitability requires from managers to find new revenue sources.

Surprise subscriptions offer a particularly large number of additional revenue mechanisms. They can provide consumer goods manufacturers with valuable market research information. Surprise subscription providers can, for example, collect customer feedback on certain sample products contained in the box and then forward this feedback to the producer as a market study. Especially before market launch, such channels can be highly relevant for consumer goods manufacturers if subscribers match the company's target group. However, cooperation between surprise subscriptions and consumer goods companies is not without challenges. Subscription providers should be cautious about the temptation to sell product placements in their subscription box. Such practices, if disclosed, could undermine consumer confidence in the surprise mechanism.

Since all subscribers to a surprise subscription usually receive identical boxes, providers can pursue customer retention through community building. Online forums or conferences allow customers to exchange information on an existing product range. That communal experience intensifies the subscription experience and increases customer loyalty.

4.2.6 Check for success

Sixth, subscription success can be monitored by maintaining several KPIs. We distinguish general (i.e., cross-type) and specific (i.e., type-specific) key figures. Regardless of subscription type, the most important general performance indicators relate first to the profit generated by every dispatched subscription box and second to the growth rate of the customer base. Subscription providers should not lose money by selling a subscription box per se, unless other revenue sources can offset that loss. Growth is critical to the valuation of a business and important for the willingness to continue investing in subscription expansion.

The cross-type level involves other customer-related performance indicators: customer acquisition costs, customer retention rate, and customer lifetime value. The first indicator measures the advertising and discounting costs required to acquire new customers. It is also important to use the retention rate to monitor how long customers remained subscribed. This enables determining a customer's lifetime value. This indicator corresponds to a customer's contribution margin during his or her subscription. In turn, this key figure enables estimating the highest possible customer acquisition costs that a provider can afford to incur to profitably acquire new customers. As shown, Blacksocks is willing to invest customer acquisition costs equal to the contribution margin in the first year to acquire new customers. This example illustrates the focus on the long-term profitability of customer relationships.

On a type-specific level, a subscription provider can establish additional revenue sources in addition to subscription box profits. For example, revenues from online shop cross-selling, community events, or market studies (commissioned by producers), and even product placements can positively impact the profitability of subscription services. Overall, as many conceivable subscription revenue sources as possible should be combined to increase profitability (see Section 4.1.2 for a description of type-specific additional revenue sources).

These six steps form the basis for future subscription providers to participate in this disruptive yet growing form of retail.

4.3 Excursion: The importance of managing subscribers' anticipation

If you have made it up to this point, dear reader, you deserve that we let you in on a little secret. You might remember that subscription managers altogether struggle with their arch nemesis: churn – or, in other terms, retention. All too many subscribers turn out to be one-off purchasers not willing to keep up their subscription beyond the shortest subscription length offered by subscription providers. In this chapter, we highlight a means that we have found, in preliminary laboratory and field experiments, to make a significant difference in subscription managers' ability to reduce churn and simultaneously increase retention by increasing subscribers' satisfaction and perceived value with a subscription service.

Subscription providers focus all too much on one single moment of truth, namely the packages sent out with each delivery, while they neglect to make use of a much longer period of moments of truth: the idle cycle between deliveries. As large portions of the subscription economy send their deliveries on a regular (e.g., monthly or quarterly) basis, we marveled at the fact that subscription providers rarely supercharge idle cycles with emotions by driving pleasant anticipation through pre-announcements of future deliveries.

As an example, let us consider the case of a surprise subscription sending out monthly boxes with vanguard beauty items. Now let us imagine the customer experience of subscribers to this service. After purchasing the subscription, they eagerly await their first deliveries, having previously heard about the service's excellent offering via media outlets and word-of-mouth. For the sake of argument, let us assume the first two deliveries are to the subscribers' fullest satisfaction. With more and more beauty products piling up in subscribers' bathrooms, however, they will inevitably reconsider whether they really need yet another delivery or whether they should take a break from the subscription – the point at which many subscribers opt for a cancellation. But what if the subscription provider had sent out a teaser e-mail with a partial pre-announcement of selected items to be included in the next delivery? Could that not have convinced a few subscribers at the brink of cancellation to stay and make their mind up only after the next delivery?

It is assumed that not everybody is equally accepting of surprise as a subscription mechanism, as would be the case with the above-mentioned example of the surprise subscription of beauty products. While many consumers might be thrilled to try out such a service, some might end up realizing that surprises are not for them, meaning that they want to control which products they purchase and consume. Given that many consumer goods subscriptions apply a surprise or a curation mechanism, rendering these subscriptions more of a nice-to-have than an essential purchase, it is important to equip subscription managers with a way to keep subscribers at it. But how can subscribers be convinced not to cancel their subscription?

The secret lies in extending a subscription's value: from providing excellent subscription boxes to providing emotional value in the form of savoring an upcoming delivery. Intermittent time periods, in which consumers wait for an upcoming consumption experience, thus represent untapped potential for subscription managers. Recent efforts in anticipation-related research have identified the value of anticipation management. Customers' savoring of an upcoming experience, such as a hotel stay, was found to have a positive impact on ongoing and remembered enjoyment, ergo satisfaction overall.

Savoring in terms of subscriptions can, according to our research, be induced by reducing the realm of possibilities and thus rendering an upcoming surprise more concrete. For example, by pre-announcing some parts of the subscription or by prompting subscribers to imagine the consumption of the surprise item (e.g., "Visualize yourself cooking a delicious meal"), subscription managers can make subscribers look forward to the upcoming surprise delivery and savor the wait time up to that point.

Across three laboratory experiments (Bischof, Boettger, Rudolph, and Lehmann, 2020; Bischof, Boettger, and Rudolph, 2019) – where we asked consumers to rate a surprise recipe they would receive as part of an imaginative recipe subscription service called "Grocerée" – we found that consumers cannot look forward to a general surprise, because their mental visualization is too abstract ("The recipe could be anything," "Anything could be in the box"). Conversely, if subscribers knew what select few items the next recipe or subscription delivery included, the mental imagery in subscribers' minds would be more concrete, allowing them to savor the upcoming delivery. Consumers who were prompted with a pre-notification to visualize the consumption of their upcoming surprise recipe – while still unaware of what recipe they were about to receive – showed a willingness to pay that was significantly higher, about 39 percent higher, than their counterparts who had not been exposed to a pre-notification but similarly had to wait for one minute to retrieve their surprise recipe ($4.70 versus $3.38) (Bischof, 2019). Although this result stems from a laboratory environment – meaning that the introduction of pre-notifications prior to delivery will not directly lead to an increase of consumers' willingness to pay to the extent of roughly 40 percent – it does indeed illustrate that anticipation management improves the user experience to an extent that can have a drastic impact on key performance figures such as subscriber churn.

Prompting consumers to imagine the eventual surprise increases tension by limiting vagueness and thus summons feelings of pleasant anticipation, allowing for savoring. Providers of general surprise subscriptions must closely manage the anticipation period, during which consumers wait for the arrival of a surprise box, as this phase is crucial in increasing imagination-driven pleasant anticipation that eventually leads to increased enjoyment of the surprise box.

This is why the authors of this book have coined the concept of Anticipated Surprises. Those are defined as the deliberate purchase and anticipation of surprise items. Across two field experiments with Germany's largest gin-subscription provider, namely Liquid Director, we found support for our theoretical constructs (Bischof, 2019). In these experiments, we divided several hundreds of Liquid Director's subscribers into two groups: one that would just receive the monthly surprise gin box and one that would receive a pre-announcement of the general motive of the upcoming subscription delivery via e-mail. Measuring consumers' responses before and after the delivery, we were able to show that higher levels of savoring, induced by pre-announcements of upcoming deliveries, led to increased pleasant anticipation and, consequently, higher satisfaction with the subscription service. This in turn has the potential to reduce churn and increase satisfaction (Bischof, 2019), in line with existing theories on consumer loyalty (Bischof, Boettger, Rudolph, and Lehmann, 2020; Bischof, Boettger, and Rudolph, 2019).

The Imagination, Tension, Prediction, Reaction, and Appraisal (ITPRA) theory by David Huron (2006), forming the basis of our concept of Anticipated Surprises, shows how experiencing a surprise affects consumers' emotions. It describes the sequence of procedural emotions that occur before, during, and after a surprising instance, as detailed in Figure 4.2. It shows how the five stages of imagination, tension, prediction, reaction, and appraisal can be separated into two categories, namely pre-outcome and post-outcome responses. These two response realms happen before and after the surprising event, in our case the package delivery of Liquid Director's monthly gin subscription.

The strong effects of experiencing a surprise can be attenuated if the degree of unpredictability is manipulated. This means that more or less predictable and unpredictable events have effects of varying magnitudes on consumers' emotions. Since surprises may not be appealing to everybody, imagination and anticipation stimulation could increase the enjoyment of surprises for everybody. This means that making consumers look forward to a consumption experience increases their affective response and subsequent positive evaluation of that experience. The recurring nature of subscriptions especially calls for an implementation of mechanisms driving savoring and, subsequently, satisfaction.

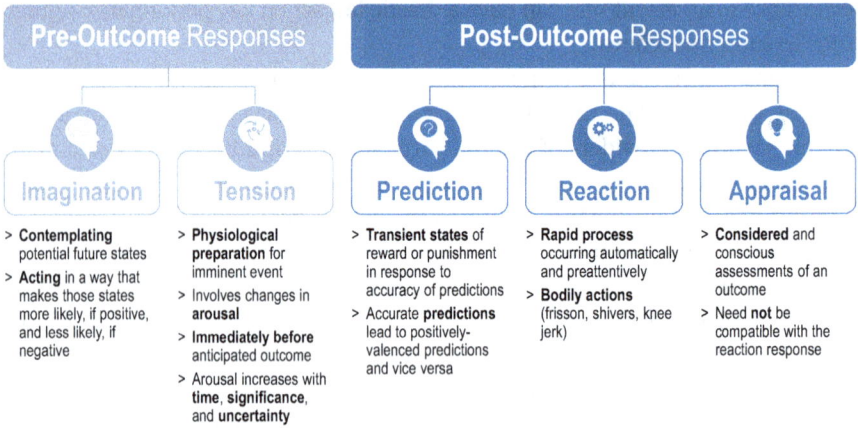

Pre-Outcome Responses		Post-Outcome Responses		
Imagination	**Tension**	**Prediction**	**Reaction**	**Appraisal**
> **Contemplating** potential future states	> **Physiological preparation** for imminent event	> **Transient states** of reward or punishment in response to accuracy of predictions	> **Rapid process** occurring automatically and preattentively	> **Considered** and conscious assessments of an outcome
> **Acting** in a way that makes those states more likely, if positive, and less likely, if negative	> Involves changes in **arousal**	> Accurate **predictions** lead to positively-valenced predictions and vice versa	> **Bodily actions** (frisson, shivers, knee jerk)	> Need **not** be compatible with the reaction response
	> **Immediately before** anticipated outcome			
	> Arousal increases with **time**, **significance**, and **uncertainty**			

Figure 4.2: Emotions in the process of anticipation.
Source: Huron (2006)

5 Case studies: Prime examples of the international subscription industry

This book has laid out the foundation for consumer goods subscriptions, with a focus on the successful conception and retailing of box retails. As a means of retailing products to consumers, it is understandable why e-commerce players have embraced this phenomenon first. The cascade then ran down to offline retailers, such as Sephora, adding subscriptions to their offering, crafting an omni-channel experience. Those farthest from the consumer, namely producers of fast-moving consumer goods, have seen a means in subscriptions to reach consumers directly. Inspired by direct-to-consumer-channels, this is the next frontier for subscriptions. Lastly, B2B subscriptions will switch to a pay-per-use model.

5.1 B2C subscription (retailer): HelloFresh

Retailers, regardless of whether their focus lies on brick-and-mortar or online operations, constantly experiment with new forms to increase revenue and profitability. Permanently pressured by intense competition and thin margins, improvement via innovations is the only way to survive. Therefore, it is understandable why pure-play retailers have started to engage in the subscription economy much earlier than, say, producers of consumer goods. In the following case study, we will describe how one such retailer, namely HelloFresh, set out to revolutionize grocery shopping by maximizing consumers' convenience.

5.1.1 General consumer need

Perhaps the greatest advantage of subscriptions is their quality of eliminating consumers' worries about making purchases for a certain category. By automating consumption, subscriptions provide a way for consumers to make sure they are always equipped with the products they require – something that consumers came to appreciate with the onset of the Covid-19 pandemic.

During the pandemic, consumers were unsure whether they could cover their needs with respect to grocery and household items. The concerns intensified, leading to panic buying (Rudolph, Bischof, Linzmajer, Kralle, and Barth, 2020). Subscriptions to meal-kits, promising the regular delivery of ingredients for meals, perfectly satisfied consumers' interest to assure the basic supply of food.

https://doi.org/10.1515/9783110730197-005

5.1.2 Company and value proposition

A subscription company that particularly excelled during this time was Hello-Fresh, a provider of curated meal-kit subscriptions. The company's value proposition, however, is special in two ways. One might think that the subscription mechanism is already successful in convincing consumers, given that that mechanism provides consumers with a basic basket of weekly groceries necessary to cook meals. But what sets HelloFresh apart is its inspiration mechanism that gives consumers new ideas on a weekly basis to expand their choice of meals. So, while consumers appreciated the regularity with which they receive groceries, it is well imaginable that many of them kept their subscription even after lockdowns due to the subscription's inspiration mechanism.

5.1.3 Financial development

Markets came to appreciate HelloFresh's value proposition in times of a pandemic. After all, HelloFresh's stock gained 135 percent in the year from March 2020 to March 2021. Guaranteeing access to food and, in a wider sense, nutrition became increasingly important to consumers, coming from a world of abundance. This might suggest that all meal-kits companies grew throughout the various lockdowns that happened globally. HelloFresh's biggest competitor Blue Apron, however, represents a black swan – its stock fell by 34 percent across the same time horizon.

Meal-kit companies, in general, fight for customers such that their success can be measured, among others, by customer acquisition costs – the cost to acquire one new customer. With HelloFresh outperforming Blue Apron on the former, paying only c.$35 [Q3, 2020] vs. c.$95 [last reported numbers, 2016], markets merely mirror the operational differences between both companies. Thus, higher demand in a pandemic, if operations are so unprofitable, logically cannot generate more money in Blue Apron's pocket.

The second differentiating factor is customer retention – the ability to keep a subscriber in business, consequently paying for the company's services. HelloFresh is deemed to be better at retaining their customers than Blue Apron, which exacerbates Blue Apron's problems: "The company is losing customers and new ones aren't making up the loss" (Sherman, 2019). In terms of customer experience, it seems that HelloFresh can excite its subscribers to a greater extent. Recipes of quickly prepared dishes written in plain language attract not only experienced cooks but also beginners. The less exotic meals (e.g., compared to those offered by Blue Apron) make HelloFresh a suited meal-kit provider for the vast majority of mainstream cooks. All this speaks in favor of HelloFresh's superior financial performance over key competitors.

5.1.4 Conclusion

Overall, HelloFresh successfully established itself as the go-to meal-kit provider with a huge selection of dishes. Endless variety and a seamless customer experience enable hobby chefs to recurrently integrate new tastes into their eating routines. Despite HelloFresh's growing market share, the meal-kit market does not appear to become a winner-takes-it-all one. Due to weak network effects, low multi-homing costs, and heterogenous customer preferences (e.g., Blue Apron for more advanced and exotic international dishes) in the meal-kit industry, more than one provider could possibly thrive in the long run.

5.2 B2C subscription (producer): Coca-Cola Insiders Club

Fast-moving consumer goods companies also take a strong interest in establishing their own subscription models. This interest is motivated in their quest to establish direct paths to their consumers. Generally, they do not directly interact with consumers, with their only access channels being the advertisements they run in the media and occasional customer feedbacks played back by the very retailers selling their products. Established fast-moving consumer goods firms now see a means of establishing a direct line to consumers by running proprietary subscription services.

Consumer goods companies' historic focus on working with retailers rather than with consumers has recently been challenged. Innovative startups, such as MyMuesli.com with their mass-customized cereals or Lizza with their low-carb pizza dough, tend to start their journey by promoting and selling their products via proprietary webstores or social media networks. Only later do they consider regular retailers as cooperation partners to widen their footprint. Of course, by that time they have already garnered so much customer feedback and built such a loyal customer base that they are perfectly in touch with their end market.

As described in our subscription implementation framework, there are many advantages consumer goods firms can derive from subscriptions. With subscriptions, they can receive direct feedback regarding their own products and get a feel for future trends by testing out innovations. Hence subscriptions provide a means for consumer goods companies to grab a hold of the retail-dominated bastion of selling to and engaging with consumers. The following case study will shed a light on consumer goods companies that employ subscription models to directly get in touch with consumers and users on a global level.

5.2.1 General consumer need

Coca-Cola highlights its customer-centricity, constantly innovating and developing products and services on behalf of customers. Jumping on the trend of D2C subscription services allows Coca-Cola to satisfy customers' desire of "choice, convenience and customization" (Coca-Cola, 2019). Coca-Cola Insiders Club's launch did target the brand's most loyal customers highly benefiting from early access to a variety of innovative drinks such as Coca-Cola Energy. At the launch of the subscription, only 1,000 membership slots were available and only US residents were eligible to subscribe. Within three hours, all slots were sold out (Coca-Cola, 2019). Simultaneously, the company benefits from additional feedback channels with customers.

5.2.2 Company and value proposition

Global giant Coca-Cola has offered iconic beverages since 1892, including the iconic Coca-Cola drink, Sprite, and Innocent juice. Initially launched as a pilot project in late 2019, Coca-Cola's Insiders Club offers fans of the brand exclusive access to nostalgic as well as innovative soft drinks before anyone else can purchase the products. Each monthly box includes a mix of new flavors and relaunched historic soft drinks as well as collectible goodies such as limited-edition Coca-Cola stickers. Even though the possible realm of products is somewhat confined to beverages and food items from within Coca-Cola's environment, subscribers never fully know what their next package will include. As such, Coca-Cola's Insiders Club represents a surprise subscription.

5.2.3 Financial development

The current form of Coca-Cola's Insiders Club will unlikely have a significant and immediate direct impact on Coca-Cola's revenue. With only 1,000 exclusive subscribers in 2020 and 2021 each, Coca-Cola Insiders Club has generated about $100,000 in revenue. The first 6-month run in 2020 contributed $50,000 to $60,000 (1,000 subscribers times $50–$60, depending on chosen payment option), and the second one running for 3 months in 2021 added $45,000 (1,000 subscribers times $45) to the total revenue. The success of the program, however, should not be measured by contributions in terms of additional revenues but by contributions in terms of direct relationships with key customers, allowing Coca-Cola to tailor their market offering ever more precisely to consumers' preferences.

Based on direct customer and social media feedback, Coca-Cola aims to cherry pick subscribers' favorites and filter out those products that do not resonate well with consumers before they hit mass markets' shelves. Additionally, the lean launch of the Insiders Club enables the company to learn from a small batch of loyal customers which features of the subscription program are highly valued and which need to be reassessed to form a fully convincing value proposition.

5.2.4 Conclusion

Coca-Cola's experiment in setting up a subscription service illustrates how entrepreneurial methods represent a means to transform incumbent firms, at the very least making them more consumer focused. As of early 2021, the Insider Club's main goal is not financial success through membership revenues but rather to learn what customers appreciate in terms of product assortment and subscription design. So far, Coca-Cola's Insiders Club has not been rolled out to the mass market. Coca-Cola, however, already announced its plans to eventually expand its service and provide access to the broader customer base in case of success (Coca-Cola, 2019). Future expansions are likely and will make Coca-Cola an even more customer-centric company.

5.3 B2C subscription (producer): Porsche Drive

5.3.1 General consumer need

Pay-per-use models are increasingly gaining a foothold in former ownership-oriented markets such as automotive. New consumer preferences, driven by an orientation around personal flexibility, have benefited the emergence of car subscriptions. These car subscriptions provide a hassle-free alternative to car ownership, covering everything from insurance, licensing, and tax to service, maintenance, and repairs. With this move, automotive firms push their forward integration, entering the premises formerly covered entirely by insurance firms; bold move or destined to fail?

Many millennials (anyone born from 1981 to 1996) and especially the so-called Generation Z (anyone born from 1997 to 2012) value ownership over physical things less than previous generations did. The car loses its role as status symbol and the number of driver license registrations has gone down (Cosmos-Direkt, 2020). Instead, younger generations demand high flexibility, rigorous personalization, as well as simplicity from mobility solutions. These younger consumers want to be able to flexibly adapt according to their current personal circumstances as well as planned occasions, which may change frequently. This shift in preferences is a consequence of today's dynamic world, where especially personal parameters, such as residence and job requirements, are subject to rapid changes.

Owning a car – in the case of Porsche even a luxurious one – does not fit these young, urban consumers' lifestyles anymore, literally being driven away from long-term commitments not only in terms of their relationships with home ownership and their interpersonal relationships but also relationships with cars. As a response, Porsche introduced Porsche Drive, a subscription aimed at pulling consumers into its ecosystem through lowering barriers to entry. After all, with many young consumers unable to finance home ownership, buying a luxury sports car might rather seem like a distant dream than a fruitful pursuit. Porsche thus offers a way for consumers to experience its brand without the full-on commitment to finance and own a sports car, but to get to know the brand one step at a time.

5.3.2 Company and value proposition

Porsche positions its subscription service between short-term renting (usage of hours and days) and the traditional leasing offerings (minimum commitment of 12 months). With Porsche's predefined subscription scheme, customers receive instantaneous access to more than 20 different car models of the company, from the Porsche Macan to the iconic Porsche 911. All are used cars aged from six to 48 months. For a fixed monthly fee, depending on the chosen model, subscribers receive a comfortable all-in-one package, consisting of the chosen car, necessary insurance, and maintenance fees, such as swapping summer for winter wheels and vice versa. As such, the experience got simplified and additional expenses are limited to individual fuel costs. After the contractual minimum period of six months, customers have the flexibility to cancel the subscription contract or to switch among car models if current needs have changed by submitting their request three months in advance. As such, hitting clear roads in a fast Porsche 911 during spring, after snowy winter months with a Porsche Cayenne, will only be possible if the subscriber submits the change request in time and has been enrolled for at least six months at the day the current car should get exchanged. Switching cars is possible every three months, even across price categories (Porsche, 2021). Jumping from a Cayenne to a Porsche 911 may increase the monthly subscription fee from €2,300 to more than €2,900 since that fee varies and depends on the currently chosen model. Porsche's operating advantages lie in the huge carpool of its already existing short-term rental and leasing services as well as its established retail footprint with its many Porsche Centers fostering efficient distribution.

5.3.3 Financial development

Porsche's subscription service launched at the end of 2020's third quarter. By April 2021, Porsche had not published any financial data for its subscription service, but the car manufacturer had shared that 80 percent of US-subscribers are new Porsche customers with many younger than the average Porsche customer. As such, Porsche celebrates the subscription's early days already as a success, as the company has been able to expand its customer network (Porsche, 2020).

5.3.4 Conclusion

Automobile subscriptions allow subscribers to drive an SUV in winter and to enjoy a convertible in summer without even owning a single car. With its predefined subscription, Porsche aims to enroll the young generation into its ecosystem. While preliminary data from the US market show promising results, it remains to be seen how quickly the car subscription scheme will catch on in other economies and demographics. For the moment, however, Porsche's current endeavors will render worthwhile in terms of engaging with and learning more about consumers' shifting preferences.

Right before the publication of this book, car subscriptions gained further momentum. Beside many upspringing independent subscription providers, Mercedes has joined the game. It becomes clear that car producers' verticalization and forward integration – by offering license plates, insurance, and repairs along with a car – proves a promising path to increase their capture rate of consumers otherwise not willing to become car owners.

Pricing-wise, however, Mercedes expects that customers hone this all-in-one carefree package with a premium in their willingness to pay. For a Mercedes A-Class, customers are asked to pay in the region of CHF 1,150 per month.

At a minimum subscription length of 6 months, this offering seems like a starting offer to test the market for car subscriptions. Long term, it can be expected that such models will allow for more short-term subscriptions of, for example, about 3 months. This would widen the realm of potential customers by a great deal. Attracting short-term subscribers, however, might lead to a deterioration of utilization per car in the producer's carpool. Eventually, Mercedes and Porsche will have to decide whether this subscription can be profitable on its own or whether it can be used as a tool – similar to Porsche's efforts – to take consumers by the hand toward their first experiences with their brand, eventually transforming them into followers and, eventually, buyers.

5.4 B2B subscription (producer): GreenMNKY

It would be incomplete to only consider consumer-focused subscriptions in this book. B2B companies are increasingly focused on establishing subscription models when selling to other companies. Many companies selling heavy machinery, such as TRUMPF or Hilti, are not selling the direct products they produce, but rather the hours or minutes by which their corporate customers use these machines. This means that B2B companies are increasingly switching from one-off sales to usage-dependent sales. A prime example for this is Rolls-Royce, which does not sell its airplane turbines but rather leases them to airline companies, charging them by the hour flown. This development has been ongoing for the past two decades. Now, this subscription thinking is spilling over from heavy industrial appliances to smaller consumer-focused machines. The next case on GreenMNKY showcases this development excellently.

5.4.1 General consumer need

Roughly 80 percent of all citizens living in Germany, UK, and USA own and use nowadays at least one smartphone (Newzoo, 2020). With several hundreds of new smartphone models released every year and an average replacement period of about 3.2 years (Morgan Stanley, 2020), it is unlikely the global conquest of smartphones will halt anytime soon, continuously capturing significant spending from consumers.

Smartphone owners know all too well about the fragility of their precious phones, costing more than $1,000 for some of the latest models, and seek to protect them quite literally "at all cost", acquiring all means possible, from screen protectors and display covers to external bumpers, sleeves, and pop sockets. For illustration, the global smartphone protective case market alone amounted to a market size of $21.4 billion in 2019 and keeps growing steadily with a compound annual growth rate (CAGR) of 6.5 percent (Research and Markets, 2020). The overall smartphone accessories market, including the likes of screen protectors and headphones, is estimated to be in the region of about $229 billion (Research and Markets, 2020) and – due to the constant influx of new phone models – becomes ever more attractive for companies helping retailers get a grip on the complexity in serving their consumers.

5.4.2 Company and value proposition

GreenMNKY set out to help retailers cope with the complexity in the smartphone accessories market. With decades of experience as shop owners selling mobile phones and phone contracts, Ziya Orhan and his co-founders created a solution that would help retailers offer the right piece of smartphone accessory – screen protectors in the case of GreenMNKY – to every customer entering a store.

Shop owners usually lament four problems:
- They are required to keep a large stock of different smartphone accessories, especially screen protectors, in order to serve customers. Keeping screen protectors in every form and shape in stock takes up valuable space in phone shops, negatively impacting KPIs such as returns per square-foot.
- Screen protectors represent an environmental hazard, as every screen protector comes with a consumer-facing packaging, ergo leading to lots of waste.
- Some smartphone models might be "too" new, such that shop owners have not yet had a chance to procure screen protectors to sell to early adopters.
- Worst comes to worst, some screen protectors may expire, meaning that they are not relevant any more, given that their corresponding smartphone becomes outdated.

GreenMNKY's solution, however, does away with all three problems. Their machine – the so-called Ape 1 – enables retailers to "print" screen protectors for every smartphone model on the spot by cutting raw pieces of protective glass into shape to exactly fit the screen they are being put on. The database with "printable" protector formats is updated regularly to offer every shape in demand. Retailers equipped with an Ape 1, thus, need not keep a large inventory of various types of screen protectors for the many smartphone types in circulation but only as many pieces of raw protective glass as the number of customers they forecast to serve. As a result, retailers require much less storage space in their stores, partially due to the absence of consumer packaging, which improves their overall ecological balance reducing waste. Finally, GreenMNKY's value proposition, thus, is the ability to help retailers avoid losing valuable customers, who enter their stores with a clear intent to purchase a screen protector, because the right screen protector is currently not in stock.

5.4.3 Financial development

The founders have landed one of the biggest deals in the history of Germany's TV show *The Lion's Den* (*Die Höhle der Löwen*), receiving about $400,000 from the grand seigneur of Germany's venture capital (VC) society Carsten Maschmeyer and the coveted serial entrepreneur Nils Glagau in exchange for 24 percent of their company. VC-funded and privately owned, financial performance data is currently not available for GreenMNKY. However, the founders have provided us with detailed information on their economies.

The cutter would cost about $500, but GreenMNKY maintains full ownership of the devices and provides it to retailers free of charge as long as they uphold a subscription to raw screen protector pieces. Hence, retailers including the GreenMNKY offering in their stores do not have any up-front costs, making this offer very appealing. In addition, GreenMNKY equips their B2B customers with marketing material valued at $250 to allow for an appealing representation of the firm and technology at the point of sale. Their initial up-front cost, ergo their investment in a B2B customer, thus, aggregates to €750.

With such significant pre-investments for the coverage of just one point of sale, GreenMNKY clearly portrays a strategy based on customer lifetime value, aiming to reach profitability through a long-term relationship with customers. This is exhibited in their pricing model. Retailers subscribe to GreenMNKY's subscription, receiving a certain number of raw screen protector pieces on a monthly basis. It is then the retailer's responsibility to attract enough customers to sell the regularly incoming screen protectors. Each display cover costs Green-MNKY approximately $2 to produce. Sold to B2B customers at about $4 reveals a 100 percent margin top-up. With $2 earned per display protection, one customer would reach the break-even point after 375 displays covers. After selling 100 screen protectors with the initial provision of the screen cutter machine, GreenMNKY expects to sell from 50 to 100 screen protectors per B2B customer per month, reaching the break-even point per customer already within the first half or full year.

Profitability, however, is subject to reaching a critical mass of paying subscribers. Adopting new retailers too fast could increase pre-investments without running subscriptions generating enough cash flow to justify the up-front investments. This exemplifies the significant risks involved in creating subscription-based business models, as they will only work if customers stay customers beyond the break-even point. Therefore, an excellent after-sales service and ongoing sales and marketing support are crucial in building a solid B2B customer base to sustain profitable growth.

On a sidenote, GreenMNKY's pricing model also aspires to embrace the tenets of the Circular Economy, a principle in which participants within an economy aim at eliminating waste, allowing the continual use of resources. By maintaining ownership of all Ape 1 cutters, GreenMNKY has the ability to take back devices from retailers who no longer uphold a subscription, refurbish them and hand them out to newly acquired customers. This reduces idle resources and, accordingly, reduces the carbon footprint of the company.

5.4.4 Conclusion

GreenMNKY had a choice: either selling the Ape 1, their screen protector cutting machine, or selling the ability to sell a screen protector for every possible smartphone on the planet. The company chose the latter, embracing the fundamental idea of subscriptions, to nurture long-term customer relationships, instead of one-off purchases enabling continuing purchases. Overall, this might be the essence of what convinced major investors to join the company's conquest across Europe and beyond: their ability to create stable cash flows by providing a solution that makes both retailers' and consumers' lives easier, all while embracing ecological concerns.

6 Outlook

Subscriptions and automated trading represent technology-based revenue model innovations. Importantly, they can create added value for customers and companies in the digital age. Marketers are constantly looking for innovative ways to simplify or emotionalize consumer shopping. Our book shows that subscriptions serve both purposes. It also provides models and guidance that enable managers to develop value-creating subscriptions: more convenience or more inspiration, or indeed both. We thus support the ongoing emphasis of marketing research on a customer-centric approach to designing experience and service processes (Chase and Dasu, 2001; Dixon, Victorino, Kwortnik, and Verma, 2017). Overall, our book marks a first step toward better understanding subscriptions and aims to stimulate their development in the market.

In times when classical retail is under very strong pressure, it is more urgent than ever to focus on aspects that make the difference. In particular personalization and one-to-one marketing will become increasingly important. Hence, implementing subscriptions is a viable option for managers. A central focus of automation and personalization must be data protection. Subscriptions allow retailers to gain deep insights into consumers' need structures and buying experiences. The outsourcing of purchasing authority associated with automation requires a high level of trust in subscription providers. Such trust is essential for both customer acquisition and retention.

Subscriptions are able to satisfy both utilitarian and hedonic needs. They might even satisfy both needs simultaneously, offering providers the chance to enhance their attractiveness. Ideally, this will lead to increased satisfaction, more loyalty, and a higher share of wallet. It should be remembered that with improved logistics, predefined subscriptions in particular could offer a frictionless shopping experience. Subscriptions could then spread at the expense of one-time purchases. This would have implications especially for stationary retailers. However, do not cling to your existing business model, but embrace the possibilities of subscription services.

https://doi.org/10.1515/9783110730197-006

Key takeaways

- Product subscriptions are already widespread, increasing their footprint across industries and product categories and into both B2C and B2B environments.
- From the consumer's perspective, the four basic subscription types (Predefined, Curated, Surprise, Access) differ significantly in their surprise and personalization character, as well as the associated controllability of the delivered products.
- Subscribers tend to be younger people and have a higher gross household income. They see themselves as experts within their subscription categories, tend to be more willing to take risks, and consider shopping to be more of an adventure.
- Established retailers do not yet have their own subscriptions – the scene is currently dominated by small start-ups. This opens up opportunities for new subscription providers.
- Subscription providers should increase their profitability through complementary revenue sources. For example, depending on the subscription type, they can:
  - operate online shops in order to benefit from cross-selling effects
  - sell consumer reviews to consumer goods manufacturers and thus develop their customer base into a lead user channel
  - establish communities to increase customer lifetime value
- A central requirement is a convincing value proposition that inspires customers. Providers lacking such a proposition should not consider establishing subscriptions.

https://doi.org/10.1515/9783110730197-007

About the authors

Severin Bischof is Senior Consultant at Roland Berger and former postdoctoral researcher and project manager at the University of St. Gallen (HSG). He was a Swiss National Science Foundation fellow at the marketing department of Columbia Business School in New York City and received his PhD from the Institute of Retail Management at the University of St. Gallen (IRM–HSG) for his dissertation on *Subscription Commerce: Theoretical, Behavioral, and Managerial Implications of Surprise as a Retail Mechanism* (2019). His research on consumer and management-specific aspects of subscriptions and automated retailing have been featured in major scientific and managerial outlets (e.g., *Journal of Retailing and Consumer Services*, *Marketing Review St. Gallen*, *Harvard Business Manager*, and *Brand Eins*). He studied business administration at the University of St. Gallen, Harvard University, Universidad Adolfo Ibáñez (Adolfo Ibáñez University), and the London School of Economics. His previous work experiences include Google, Procter & Gamble, Deloitte, and Li & Fung.

Thomas Rudolph is a professor of Business Administration and Marketing and director of the Institute of Retail Management at the University of St. Gallen (IRM HSG). He holds the Gottlieb Duttweiler Chair of International Retail Management and heads the St. Gallen Retail Lab, which brings scientific findings closer to practice in the form of research workshops, courses, and certificate programs. He was a visiting professor at Brigham Young University in Utah (1998), at the University of Florida (2001), at ESADE in Barcelona (2006), and at Massey University in Auckland (2008). Thomas Rudolph is the author of more than 10 books and more than 350 articles on marketing and retail topics in renowned journals such as the *Journal of Marketing*, the *Journal of Retailing*, the *Journal of the Association for Consumer Research*, and the *Harvard Business Manager*. He maintains close contact with the media and the business world in his capacity as a board member of renowned international companies, as a coach, and as a retail management expert.

https://doi.org/10.1515/9783110730197-008

References

Baxter, R. K. (2015): The Membership Economy: Find Your Super Users, Master the Forever Transaction, and Build Recurring Revenue. McGraw-Hill.

Berg, N. and Knights, M. (2019). *Amazon: How the World's Most Relentless Retailer Will Continue to Revolutionize Commerce.* New York: Kogan Page.

Bischof, S. F. (2019). *Subscription Commerce: Theoretical, Behavioral, and Managerial Implications of Surprise as a Retail Mechanism.* Dissertation, the University of St. Gallen.

Bischof, S. F., Boettger, T. M., and Rudolph, T. (2017). Cautiousness Caps Curiosity: The Influence of Risk on Attitude towards Product Subscription Models. *European Marketing Academy (EMAC) 46th Annual Conference,* Groningen, Netherlands.

Bischof, S. F., Boettger, T. M., and Rudolph, T. (2019). Managing Customers' Imagination: Antecedents and Effects of Anticipated Surprises. *European Marketing Academy (EMAC) 48th Annual Conference,* Hamburg, Germany.

Bischof, S. F., Boettger, T. M., and Rudolph, T. (2020). Curated Subscription Commerce: A Theoretical Conceptualization. *Journal of Retailing and Consumer Services,* 54(5), 1–15.

Bischof, S. F., Boettger, T. M., Rudolph, T., and Lehmann, D. (2020). Managing Customers' Imagination: Antecedents and Effects of Anticipated Surprises. *Association for Consumer Research (ACR),* Paris, France.

Bischof, S. F. and Rudolph, T. (2020). *Subskriptionsmodelle im Handel: Wie Subskriptionen den Konsum automatisieren.* Wiesbaden: Springer Gabler, ISBN: 978–3–658–29677–3.

Bischof, S. F., Rudolph, T., and Hauschke, A. (2020). Wie Aboboxen profitabel werden. *Harvard Business Manager (HBM),* 9, 50–57.

Bischof, S. F., Rudolph, T., Scheidegger, G., and Boettger, T. M. (2018). The Cost of Convenience: How Risk Jeopardizes Convenience in Automated Shopping. *European Marketing Academy (EMAC) 47th Annual Conference,* Glasgow, Scotland.

Bischof, S. F., Scheidegger, G. Boettger, T. M., and Rudolph, T. (2019). Automated Commerce: Consumers' Tolerance for Service Failures in Agency Situations. *Theory + Practice in Marketing (TPM) 9th Annual Conference,* New York City, USA.

CB Insights. (2016). Subscription E-Commerce Market Map, 57 Startups in One Infographic. Retrieved May 1, 2021 from https://www.cbinsights.com/blog/subscription/ecommerce-market-map-company-list/

Chase, R. B. and Dasu, S. (2001). Want to Perfect Your Company's Service? Use Behavioral Science. *Harvard Business Review,* 79(6), 78–84.

Chen, T., Fenyo, K., Yang, S., and Zhang, J. (2018). Thinking Inside the Subscription Box. New Research on e-commerce Consumers. *McKinsey & Company.* Retrieved May 1, 2021 from https://www.mckinsey.com/industries/high-tech/our-insights/thinking-inside-the-subscription-box-new-research-on-ecommerce-consumers

Coca-Cola. (2019). First Taste: Coca-Cola "Insiders" Can Sign Up to Have Newest Drinks Delivered to Their Doorstep. Retrieved May 1, 2021 from https://www.coca-colacompany.com/news/first-taste-coca-cola-insiders-can-sign-up-to-have-newest-drinks-delivered

CosmosDirekt. (2020). „Generation Rücksitz": Was Fahranfänger wissen müssen. Retrieved May 1, 2021 from https://www.cosmosdirekt.de/autoversicherung/generation-ruecksitz

Cratejoy. (2018). Subscribe to What you Love. Retrieved May 1, 2021 from https://www.cratejoy.com/

https://doi.org/10.1515/9783110730197-009

Dixon, M. J., Victorino, L., Kwortnik, R. J., and Verma, R. (2017). Surprise, Anticipation, and Sequence Effects in the Design of Experiential Services. *Production and Operations Management*, 26(5), 945–960.

Grewal, D., Roggeveen, A. L., Compeau, L. D., and Levy, M. (2012). Retail Value-Based Pricing Strategies: New Times, New Technologies, New Consumers. *Journal of Retailing*, 88(1), 1–6.

Grewal, D., Roggeveen, A. L., and Nordfält, J. (2017). The Future of Retailing. *Journal of Retailing*, 93(1), 1–6.

Guentert, A. (2019, June 20). „Ikea bittet zum Büro-‚Mieting'". *Handelszeitung*. Retrieved May 1, 2021 from https://www.handelszeitung.ch/unternehmen/ikea-bittet-zum-buro-mieting

Guentert, A. (2019, June 24). „Mieten statt kaufen: So funktioniert das Möbel-Abo von Ikea". *Die Welt*. Retrieved May 1, 2021 from https://www.welt.de/wirtschaft/article195765311/Mieten-statt-kaufen-Ikea-bietet-in-der-Schweiz-Moebel-im-Abo-an.html

Guentert, A. (2020, May 7). "Ein M mutig? Migros eifert Amazon nach". *Handelszeitung*. Retrieved May 1, 2021 from https://www.handelszeitung.ch/unternehmen/ein-m-mutig-migros-eifert-amazon-nach

Guentert, A. (2020, September 11). „Jetzt gibt's den Kaffee bei der Migros im Abo". *Handelszeitung*. Retrieved May 1, 2021 from https://www.handelszeitung.ch/unterneh men/jetzt-gibts-den-kaffee-bei-der-migros-im-abo

Gupta, S., Lehmann, D. R., and Stuart, J. A. (2004). Valuing Customers. *Journal of Marketing Research*, 41(1), 7–18.

Huron, D. (2006). *Sweet Anticipation: Music and the Psychology of Expectation*. Cambridge, MA: The MIT Press.

Janzer, A. H. (2015). Strategies for Nurturing Customers in A World of Churn: Subscription Marketing. Cuesta Park Consulting.

Kessler, S. (2016, 20 October). Meal-Kit Customers Dine and Dash. *Fast Company*. Retrieved May 1, 2021 from https://www.fastcompany.com/3064792/app-economy/meal-kit-cus tomers-dine-and-dash

Kumar, V. and Reinartz, W. (2016). Creating Enduring Customer Value. *Journal of Marketing*, 80(6), 36–68. https://doi.org/10.1509/jm.15.0414

Livsey, A. (2017, March 17). Dollar Shave Club Wins Market Share and Customers with Back-to-basics Approach. *Financial Times*. Retrieved May 1, 2021 from https://www.ft.com/con tent/9bb5cc54-d368-11e6-b06b-680c49b4b4c0

Molla, R. (2017, June 8). For the Wealthiest Americans, Amazon Prime has Become the Norm. *Recode*. Retrieved May 1, 2021 from https://www.vox.com/2017/6/8/15759354/amazon-prime-low-income-discount-piper-jaffray-demographics

Morgan Stanley (2020). Will 5G Supercharge Smartphone Sales? Retrieved May 1, 2021 from https://www.morganstanley.com/ideas/5G-smartphone-growth–2020

Newzoo. (2020). Top Countries by Smartphone Users. Retrieved May 1, 2021 from https://new zoo.com/insights/rankings/top-countries-by-smartphone-penetration-and-users/

Peloton. (2019). Choose Your Bike Experience. Retrieved May 1, 2021 from https://www.onepe loton.com/

Porsche. (2019). Porsche Passport: All-inclusive, Monthly Vehicle Subscription Service. Retrieved May 1, 2021 from https://www.porschepassport.com/

Porsche. (2020). Porsche Launches New Single-vehicle Option as Subscription Programs Expand to Los Angeles. Retrieved May 1, 2021 from https://newsroom.porsche.com/en_ US/company/porsche-drive-launches-single-vehicle-subscription-21942.html

Porsche (2021). Porsche Drive Abo FAQs. Retrieved May 1, 2021 from https://www.porsche.
com/germany/motorsportandevents/porschedrive/abo/faq/

Reinartz, W. (2016). In the Future of Retail, We're Never Not Shopping. *Harvard Business
Review*. Retrieved May 1, 2021 from https://hbr.org/2016/03/in-the-future-of-retail-were-
never-not-shopping

Research and Markets. (2020). Mobile Phone Protective Cases Market Size, Market Share,
Application Analysis, Regional Outlook, Growth Trends, Key Players, Competitive
Strategies and Forecasts, 2020 To 2028. Retrieved May 1, 2021 from https://www.re
searchandmarkets.com/reports/5157317/mobile-phone-protective-cases-market-size-
market

Reuters (2020, January 16). HelloFresh Shares Jump on Stronger Than Expected 2019. *The New
York Times*. Retrieved May 1, 2021 from https://www.reuters.com/article/hellofresh-hot-
idUSL8N29L1Q1

Rudolph, T., Bischof, S. F., Boettger, T. M., and Weiler, N. (2017). Disruption at the Door: A
Taxonomy on Subscription Models in Retailing. *Marketing Review St. Gallen*, 34(5), 18–25.

Rudolph, T., Bischof, S. F., Linzmajer, M., Kralle, N., and Barth, E. (2020). *Retail Store of the
Future: Die Zukunft des kontaktlosen Einkaufens*. St. Gallen: Institute of Retail
Management at the University of St. Gallen. Retrieved May 1, 2021 from: https://www.
zuehlke.com/de/insights/kontaktloses-einkaufen-in-der-zukunft

Rudolph, T., Bischof, S. F., and Schuerch, S. (2019). *Subscription Models for Swiss Retail*.
St. Gallen: Institute of Retail Management at the University of St. Gallen. Retrieved May 1,
2021 from https://www.handelsliteratur-hsg.ch/studien/details/#cc-m-product–
11553667597

Segran, E. (2018, 17. October). Inside the $2.6 Billion Subscription Box Wars. *Fast Company*.
Retrieved May 1, 2021 from https://www.fastcompany.com/90248232/inside-the-2-6-bil
lion-subscription-box-wars

Shankar, V., and Yadav, M. S. (2011). Innovations in Retailing. *Journal of Retailing*, 87(1), 1–2.

Sherman, E. (2019). Blue Apron Has a Very Big Problem That Can Plague any Entrepreneur.
Retrieved May 1, 2021 from https://www.inc.com/erik-sherman/blue-apron-has-a-very-
big-problem-that-can-plague-any-entrepreneur.html

The Economist. (2013). Supply on Demand: Adapting to Change in Consumption and Delivery
Models. *The Economist* Intelligence Unit. Retrieved May 1, 2021 from http://www.econo
mistinsights.com/sites/default/files/EIU_Zuora_WEB_Final.pdf

The Economist (2018). The Subscription Addiction. *The Economist*, p. 58.

Warrillow, J. (2015). The automatic customer: creating a subscription business in any industry.
Portfolio Penguin.

List of figures

https://doi.org/10.1515/9783110730197-010

Glossary

Access subscription – An access subscription is a type of subscription allowing consumers access to an exclusive offering of products and services. The products and services offered by such a subscription are designed for a niche group of consumers and are only available to subscribers. Access subscriptions usually charge a membership fee to access or purchase products and services behind a paywall. While they are often not personalized, access subscriptions allow for subscribers to make their own decisions regarding which products and services to use or purchase once they have subscribed, thus reducing the level of surprise.

Anticipated surprise – An anticipated surprise is defined as the deliberate purchase and anticipation of surprise items.

Churn rate – The churn rate measures the rate of subscribers who cancel in a given time period.

Consumer behavior – Consumer behavior studies individuals, groups, and organizations and all the activities associated with the purchase, use and disposal of goods and services, and how the consumer's emotions, attitudes and preferences affect purchasing behavior.

Curated subscription – A curated subscription is a type of subscription with an offering curated by the subscription provider. Curated subscriptions take consumers' individual preferences into account when selecting the products that subscribers are to receive. Hence, they offer a personalized set of products all while allowing for variety through surprise.

Customer acquisition costs – Customer acquisition costs refer to the costs related to acquiring additional customers, in this case subscribers. It can be calculated by dividing total spend on acquiring subscribers in a given time period by the number of subscribers acquired.

Customer lifetime value – Customer lifetime value refers to the expected cumulative contribution margin over a subscriber's lifetime, taking into account customer acquisition costs (CAC) and discount rates.

Customer retention rate – Customer retention rate refers to the percentage of subscribers continuing their subscription beyond a given period (e.g., one subscription cycle, one year). It, thus, describes the percentage of subscribers who do not cancel within a given period.

Degree of personalization – The degree of personalization describes the extent to which products within a subscription are tailored to a subscriber's individual preferences and needs.

Degree of surprise – The degree of surprise describes the extent to which subscribers are unfamiliar with the products they are going to receive with a subscription prior to unboxing.

Hedonic need – Hedonic needs are emotional needs (e.g., seeking new experiences and inspiration), which contrast with functional needs (e.g., ensuring sufficient supply of goods).

KPI – A KPI (key performance indicator) serves as a quantifiable measure of performance over time for a specific objective.

Lead users – Lead users are consumers who are relatively advanced regarding their preferences and expectations towards products and services compared to wider society. They

https://doi.org/10.1515/9783110730197-011

are usually innovators trying out new products and services in categories of their interest and frequently shape the opinion of other consumers.

Physical consumer good – Physical consumer goods are physical, tangible products purchased by individuals for personal consumption (e.g., groceries, beauty products, household products).

Predefined subscription – A predefined subscription is a type of subscription with an offering entirely selected by the subscriber. As such, the degree of personalization is high and that of surprise is low as the subscriber is familiar with all products they are going to receive.

Risk – Risk relates to the feeling of uncertainty which consumers feel in situations with low or no control over a consumption experience. Risk is particularly existent in surprise subscriptions, where subscribers are unfamiliar with the products they are going to receive.

Subscriptions – Subscriptions are agreements between companies and consumers on recurring deliveries of products and services. Subscribers, thus, commit to regular payments in exchange for access to a set of defined products and services during the subscription period.

Surprise mechanism – The surprise mechanism refers to instances in which subscription providers choose the products a subscriber receives with their subscription. The higher the degree of surprise, the more autonomous the subscription providers are in their choice of products.

Surprise subscription – A surprise subscription is a type of subscription where the subscription provider autonomously selects the products subscribers are going to receive, without incorporating subscribers' individual preferences. As such, the degree of personalization is low and that of surprise is high.

Utilitarian need – Utilitarian needs are functional and transactional needs required on a regular or daily basis. Products satisfying those needs do not carry much emotional value (e.g., razor blades).

Value proposition – A value proposition summarizes the main reasons why consumers should do business with a specific company instead of another, explaining the particular company's services' or products' key benefits to its target customers.

Index

https://doi.org/10.1515/9783110730197-012

www.ingramcontent.com/pod-product-compliance
Lightning Source LLC
Chambersburg PA
CBHW061301220326
41599CB00028B/5729